Y0-BNY-043

ATE DUE

THE SANCTIFICATION CONNECTION

---

*An Exploration of Human Participation
in Spiritual Growth*

Keith Kettenring

University Press of America,® Inc.
Lanham · Boulder · New York · Toronto · Plymouth, UK

Copyright © 2008 by
University Press of America,® Inc.
4501 Forbes Boulevard
Suite 200
Lanham, Maryland 20706
UPA Acquisitions Department (301) 459-3366

Estover Road
Plymouth PL6 7PY
United Kingdom

Library of Congress Control Number: 2007933325
ISBN-13: 978-0-7618-3738-1 (paperback : alk. paper)
ISBN-10: 0-7618-3738-8 (paperback : alk. paper)

Dedicated to

*my parents, Joel and Pauline Kettenring
who modeled sanctification in
their lives and ministry*

and

*my dear wife, Rhonda, who provides the
home environment and supportive
relationship for sanctification
to take place*

CONTENTS

PREFACE

The conceptual seeds of this study were planted in me during the course of my life, but were encouraged to blossom primarily through interaction with Dr. Klaus Issler who mentored me throughout my doctoral program at Talbot School of Theology. At an orientation meeting, he stated that there was much work that needed to be done on the doctrine of sanctification. Not knowing the extent of scholarly work on this subject, I was not sure if I believed him. However, over the next six years I began to understand the truth of his statement. He also introduced me to Martin Ford's theory of motivation and Dallas Willard's writings on Christian character development. As well, his influence on me in the area of spiritual formation was significant. These resources and experiences have informed this study to a great degree.

Sanctification has been addressed by many theologians, some Bible scholars, and a handful of Christian philosophers. However, there are few works that seek to integrate concepts from these various fields resulting in a more complete picture of sanctification. This book is such an attempt. I have a growing conviction that it will take an integrative approach to the study of sanctification in order to provide a more comprehensive understanding of this vital doctrine. This book begins a journey that I hope will lead to a robust and clear picture of sanctification.

Because this book presents an integrative study, it may be confusing to some. Integration is a challenging approach to research and thus may not be understood by the reader. Instead of digging deep into a subject, integration draws salient concepts from various related fields to explore the possibility of forming a more robust picture of the subject. I have taken a model from a philosopher (Willard's VIM), a model from an educational psychologist (Ford's MST and Personal Agency Beliefs), a "model" from Scripture and theology (the Apostle Paul's "in-Christ" motif), to explore their compatibility with progressive sanctification. Please keep this in mind as you read this book. It is not an exhaustive study of sanctification, but an exploration of the coherency of these models as they relate to sanctification.

This particular study focuses on progressive sanctification wherein a divine-human synergism plays an essential role and wherein a motivational setting for the transformation of life may be provided. Human participation in God's work of sanctification is recognized through an examination of free will, a study of components that contribute to belief and character formation, and an analysis of the compatibility of Martin Ford's personal agency beliefs model with Paul's union with Christ concept and Dallas Willard's VIM model with Paul's instructions in Romans 6:1–14. The goal of this study is to arrive at a more comprehensive understanding of progressive sanctification.

The study suggests that believers participate in sanctificational synergism; a participation that includes the evaluation of one's capabilities and one's context for goal-oriented action (i.e., personal agency beliefs). These beliefs seem to provide compatible and useful components for an understanding of sanctificational growth. This motivational component is the primary contribution of this study to the discussion of sanctificational growth.

The examination of the relationship of human participation and union with Christ involves the use of two conceptual schemes. First, personal agency beliefs are integrated with the union with Christ motif to test their fit. The study suggests that it is through the deliberate evaluation of themselves in union with Christ that believers are able to find motivation for sanctificational growth. Second, Willard's VIM (vision, intention, and means) model provides a heuristic procedure for personal transformation which is integrated with Paul's sanctificational rubric of Romans 6:1–14 to test their compatibility.

Finally, some educational and ministry implications of the study center on the notions that Christian education is a synergistic endeavor and that Christians need to develop beliefs. The study of the components of human participation is applied to the believer's personal strategy for sanctificational growth as well as the church's corporate strategy to aid sanctificational growth through worship and small groups.

I want to thank Dr. Klaus Issler, Dr. Kevin Lawson, Dr. Garry DeWeese, and Dr. Moyer Hubbard for the encouragement to be a careful and diligent scholar-writer and to continue to pursue a deeper and broader understanding of sanctification. You all have been excellent models of gracious scholarship.

Keith A. Kettenring
Anaheim, CA
August, 2006

ACKNOWLEDGMENTS

God has been a gracious guide in this endeavor of deepening and broadening my heart and perspective. Whatever good has come as a result of this study is attributed to the loving kindness of a faithful Father who used many people to support me. This project, which includes essential events and key relationships that personally occurred over the past six years, is an example of some of the principles developed in this book.

A wonderful group of people in the family of Calvary Baptist Church have encouraged and supported this pursuit. Church leadership and many people stood with me in this undertaking. Some contributed financially and others encouraged me verbally. There were some who did both. To those who regularly inquired about my progress, I say, "Thank you for your ministry of encouragement." Your interest in this aspect of my life has meant so much. A special appreciation goes to Jo and Duane Shafer whose concern and interest was demonstrated in so many ways and so often. For all who prayed, accept my thank you for investing in my life. This project could not have been done without all of you.

My appreciation goes out to every member of my Ph.D. dissertation committee, Dr. Klaus Issler, Dr. Kevin Lawson, Dr. Garry DeWeese, and Dr. Moyer Hubbard. Your investment in me and this project was invaluable. However, special thanks goes to Dr. Klaus Issler, my mentor, chairman of the committee, and so much more. I have had the privilege of sitting under his teaching and guidance for six years and my life is profoundly richer for it. He has challenged, stretched, prodded, and helped me to become a better person. Thank you.

Most importantly, I dedicate this project to my wonderful family. My wife Rhonda has faithfully supported me from the first time I mentioned the possibility of further study in the hopes of broadening my heart and ministry. She sacrificed much and never uttered a complaint. She sensed the desire of my heart and shared it with me. Thank you, dear, for your love and support while I have been occupied by schooling and writing.

Our dear children, Nate and Jenna, have grown out of childhood while I was engaged in this pursuit. They understood, as best they could, why I was studying so much and supported me. Thank you for being so understanding and loving during these years of change and growth.

These supporters have been part of my belief that I had the "responsive environment" to pursue my goals. I have experienced practically the theories examined in this book. May God honor you and bless your lives.

Acknowledgments

Some notes about the book's format are necessary so the reader can better navigate through the material. When a work is cited (e.g., Demarest, 1997), the citation refers to a work in the reference list by that same author with the year of publication. In this way, the reader can find the resource for the information used in the study. This follows the APA (American Psychological Association) format for citations. There are no footnotes or endnotes since most of this kind of material was included in the text itself, again following APA format.

Finally, in a conceptual study such as this, there were many dialogue partners with whom I interacted. Primary among them was Martin Ford whose motivational model presented in *Motivating Humans* provided the unique contribution to the study. I want to thank Sage Publishing for permission to quote and summarize his motivational concepts. Special thanks is also due to NavPress, the publishers of Dallas Willard's *Renovation of the Heart* for permission to use his VIM model as the conceptual thread for this work. I admire Willard's depth of thought and clear writing style. Having met him and heard him speak on many occasions, his Christlike character is evident. Lastly, I quote Bruce Demarest primarily from his theological work entitled *The Cross and Salvation*. He also exemplifies gracious scholarship and a depth of genuine relationship with Jesus Christ.

Scripture quotations are from The Holy Bible, English Standard Version, copyright © 2001 by Crossway Bibles, a division of Good News Publishers. Used by permission. All rights reserved.

Martin E. Ford, *Motivating Humans: Goals, emotions, and personal agency beliefs* pp. 51, 73–75, 133, 134, 140, 147, Table 5.1 The MST Taxonomy of Personal Agency Belief Patterns, copyright 1992 by Sage Publications, Inc. Reprinted by Permission of Sage Publications, Inc.

Dallas Willard, *Renovation of the Hear: Putting on the character of Christ* pp. 39, 84, 86–91, 138–139, 124–125, 127, copyright 2002 by Navpress. Used by permission of NavPress – www.navpress.com. All rights reserved.

CHAPTER 1

INTRODUCTION: TWO MODELS
OF PERSONAL TRANSFORMATION

When people come to faith in Jesus Christ, there is usually an accompanying acknowledgment of the need to see their life changed. This becomes more obvious as new believers begin to study Scripture and observe many statements challenging their present way of thinking and living while inviting them to walk a new way. Occasionally, confusion occurs regarding the nature of this new life and the corresponding process of change or growth. Misunderstanding God's design of human nature or how he works with believers to accomplish a transformation of life may create such confusion.

However, a path out of this confusion can be discovered. It seems possible to develop constructive notions that clearly guide the believer to effective spiritual growth. Dallas Willard (2002) writes that "spiritual formation in Christ is an orderly process" (p. 10). "Sanctification" is the theological term used to describe this process. Therefore, there is a need to understand this orderly process by which God changes lives and fits people for his purposes. This study seeks to contribute to that understanding.

Sanctification is normally included in discussions regarding the doctrine of salvation. Its inclusion in salvation seems to provide a motivational setting for the transformation of life. For example, among the spiritual blessings of the believer in Christ is the acknowledgement of God's having chosen "us in him before the foundation of the world, that we should be holy and blameless before him" (Ephesians 1:4) (English Standard Version, 2001). New Testament scholar Harold Hoehner (2002) believes this verse teaches that the purpose of those chosen by God is to be holy and without blame reflecting God's character (p. 178). One of God's purposes in salvation is to bring about the holiness of his people in a transformation of life.

With the need to better understand the sanctificational process, this book examines God's sanctificational work of utilizing the believer's human faculties while acknowledging the intentional role of believers in this work. Evidence is presented that supports the essentiality of the believers' participation in God's work of sanctificational growth.

The desire to examine human participation in sanctification derives from three motivations. First, from a pastoral perspective, I want to help Christians navigate between their human responsibilities and God's divine efforts in sanctificational growth. Believers often struggle to find ways to deal with their own weaknesses and sin while trying to live godly lives. They understand that by God's grace and through faith they are fit for heaven. But many wonder if they are fit for kingdom living while present on earth. They hesitate to bring their human nature to the sanctificational process not understanding its new condition or its essential role. I would like to help believers understand their ability and the necessity to participate in the sanctificational process.

Second, there are many competent contributors trying to help believers understand the broad subject of sanctification perhaps resulting in some confusion about human participation in sanctification. Sanctification is currently being discussed in evangelicalism, perhaps due to a rediscovery of the teachings related to spiritual formation through the popular writings of Dallas Willard (2002), Kenneth Boa (2001), Gary Thomas (2000), Bruce Demarest (1999), Richard Foster (1998), and Robert Mulholland (1993). In the writings of Kenneth Collins (2000), Alister McGrath (1999), and Simon Chan (1998) an evangelical spirituality emerges that has also contributed to discussions about sanctification. Sanctification is also presented by David Peterson (1995) with a firm emphasis on sanctification as a definitive event.

The debate has also been stirred by two books (Gundry, 1987; Alexander, 1988), each presenting five views of sanctification resulting in seven different perspectives on the subject. Yet, each editor comments on the importance of addressing the issue of divine and human participation, the primary issue addressed in this book. Alexander (1988) states that one purpose of his book is to attempt "to coordinate the tension between God's sovereign work in holiness and the believer's obedient participation" (p. 9). Gundry (1987) also writes:

> In tracing the use of these concepts [e.g., sin, old man/new man, perfect, Spirit baptism] in the arguments and counterarguments, the student of sanctification must appreciate – as do all the authors – the need to preserve both divine sovereignty and human responsibility" (p. 8).

I want to contribute additional information, primarily through the integration of the concept of personal agency beliefs, which may help clarify the Christian's responsibility in sanctificational growth.

Third, my desire is to provide some theological clarity to the discussion. From a theological perspective, the various theories of sanctification (reviewed in chapter two) seem to contribute to the struggle to understand the doctrine. Believers hear confusing, and perhaps conflicting, messages about what they are to believe about Christian growth and how they are to live the Christian life, not realizing the theological frameworks that shape these messages. By focusing on the believer's responsibility and ability to participate, I hope to bring some clarity to the discussion.

To understand the sanctificational growth process, I examine the participation of the believer in God's work of sanctification by examining key resources provided by God, in particular, Christ's death and resurrection. I seek answers to such questions as these: Are believers to participate in their spiritual growth? Are believers capable of participating in their spiritual growth? How do the

Christians' beliefs about themselves and their environment inform their understanding and practice of sanctificational growth?

Thus, one purpose of this study is to demonstrate that human participation is essential to sanctification. This study addresses the nature of sanctificational growth by proposing an essential synergism component (i.e., both God and believers participate, detailed in chapter two) that dynamically operates within the believer. The effectiveness of spiritual growth appears to relate to an understanding this synergism component. More specifically, this study seeks to integrate an understanding of the believer's participation in sanctification and an understanding of the nature of personal agency beliefs (i.e., one's evaluative thoughts of personal capabilities and environment, detailed in chapter four) with the Pauline motif of union with Christ (detailed in chapter five) and thus lend clarity to the discussion of sanctificational motivation.

The research plan to understand the synergism component in sanctificational growth will utilize Willard's (2002) VIM (Vision, Intention, and Means) model. It provides a heuristic framework for personal transformation that includes the necessity of human participation. In chapter two, I will suggest that sanctificational synergism is supported by Scripture and by all evangelical theological traditions. In chapter three, I will engage in a philosophical discussion of the believer's capability to participate in sanctificational growth, having been endowed with free will, through the indirect means of belief and character formation. One set of beliefs that seem to contribute to sanctificational growth is personal agency beliefs, which will be examined in chapter four. What Christians believe about their personal capabilities and context has a bearing on their motivation for spiritual growth. Chapter five will provide an analysis of Paul's "union with Christ" motif and will examine the relationship that concept has with Willard's VIM model and Ford's personal agency beliefs. I want to establish an understanding of human participation in sanctificational growth, add to this understanding the concept of personal agency beliefs, and then see how these concepts integrate with the concept of union with Christ. Chapter six presents some educational and ministry implications of the study.

Methodology

Professor Steven Porter (2002) notes the present confusion in understanding key elements in contemporary discussion of sanctification and places some of the blame on the methodologies used to frame the discussion. However, he believes that "the most likely path out of the confusion . . . is *via* a systematic treatment of the doctrine of sanctification" (p. 424) meaning an analysis "related more explicitly to the doctrine of God, human nature, sin, the atonement, justification, regeneration, the indwelling of the Holy Spirit, etc." (p. 425). This study attempts to, at least in part, explore sanctification with this kind of analysis. I examine aspects of human nature, union with Christ (and the Spirit), and human participation in sanctification, all of which can be informed by theology and Scripture since sanctification is primarily a theological concept.

However, one of the contributions to the confusion regarding sanctification may be the belief that it is only a theological issue. This study suggests that sanctification entails a theological understanding of the concept but also suggests that theology is not sufficient for a comprehensive understanding. Evangelical Christian educators can contribute to an understanding of sanctification due to their commitment to orthodox theology, to integration of science and Scripture along with faith and learning, and to bridging theory and practice.

Accordingly, this book is primarily an integrative undertaking. The primary consideration is to integrate subject material from various disciplines to form a coherent perspective on human participation in sanctification. By examining concepts from science (i.e., philosophy and psychology) and from faith (i.e., theology and special revelation) and bringing them together implies that it is useful to and compatible with the goal of Christian education (Clement, 2001, p. 366). This effort to integrate faith and science is made with a commitment to truth as revealed in the Scriptures. My goal is to arrive at a more comprehensive understanding of progressive sanctification informed by science and faith.

However, by its nature, integration implies a limitation regarding the depth and breadth of analysis. As a result, the scope of this project will always be held in tension. I acknowledge that this is an imprecise process but one that seems necessary for a better understanding of the subject.

As has been implied, one characteristic of Christian education is its integration methodology. Christian educator, Kenneth Gangel (2001) ties the concepts of education and theology together when he states that integration refers to the (Christian) educational process that includes "all subjects as part of the total truth of God thereby enabling students to see the unity of natural and special revelation" (p. 366). This book draws upon concepts from various fields of study and subjects (e.g., psychology—motivation; anthropology—human nature; philosophy—free will and belief; theology—sanctificational synergism and the Holy Spirit) and suggests that a comprehensive understanding of sanctification includes these concepts.

This work is also a conceptual study with certain parameters. First, I situate the study within the broader context of sanctification. The reason for examining the concepts of human participation, free will, belief, personal agency beliefs, and union with Christ is to ascertain their contribution to the understanding and practice of sanctification. Second, I make one main claim for each chapter which is supported by experts in the various disciplines relevant to the claim. I also support each claim with relevant and reliable sources. These sources include not only primary resources but also secondary resources which are acceptable for this kind of integration task. For example, when addressing theological issues, I depend on sources from theologians and when addressing philosophical issues I rely upon philosophers. When these two fields overlap on an issue such as free will, I will include statements from experts in each field. Supporting the study of sanctification with such diverse sources suggests that God has designed sanctificational growth as an interplay of human nature, divine-human synergism, and belief and character formation.

In particular, this chapter presents two background concepts that are integral to the whole project. First, Dallas Willard's VIM model of personal transformation is presented as a heuristic framework for understanding sanctificational transformation. Second, a brief survey of the doctrine of sanctification is presented since a discussion of the major concepts is foundational and necessary for our discussion of the more detailed aspects of progressive sanctification. I also provide a brief overview of each chapter.

Two Concepts Describing Personal Transformation

In this study, two concepts of personal transformation are examined. First, a brief introduction to Dallas Willard's (2000) VIM model of personal transformation is presented. Second, an explanation of sanctification is presented.

Willard's Model of Personal Transformation

Dallas Willard's (2002) VIM (Vision, Intention, and Means) model provides a framework for this study of sanctificational growth. This model is utilized because it is a heuristic procedure that has the potential to describe sanctificational growth. It also provides support for the necessity for human participation in sanctificational growth. As Willard explains, this model outlines

> the general pattern that all effective efforts toward personal transformation—not just Christian formation—must follow. Because we are active participants in the process and what we do or do not do makes a huge difference, our efforts must be based on understanding. The degree of success in such efforts will essentially depend upon the degree to which this general pattern is understood and intentionally conformed to. (pp. 82–83)

Willard reduces the process of personal transformation to this simple acronym because he believes it forms a pattern for all change. He supports this claim with two illustrations: learning a language and following the process spelled out in "twelve-step" programs. In both cases, personal transformation takes place as 1) "a desirable state is *envisioned*," 2) "an *intention* to realize it is actuated in decision," and 3) "*means* are applied to fulfill intention...by producing the desirable state of being" (p. 84).

The VIM model, according to Willard (2002), also provides a pattern for personal spiritual transformation. For spiritual change, believers need to 1) envision life in the kingdom or living in union with Christ, 2) decide to intentionally participate in the process, and 3) implement means to live proficiently in God's kingdom (pp. 86–91).

Willard explains each element of this model.
    1. Vision of kingdom life:

> The vision that underlies spiritual (trans)formation into Christlikeness is, then, the vision of life now and forever in the range of God's ef-

fective will—that is, *partaking* of the divine nature (2 Peter 1:4, 1 John 3:1–2) through a birth "from above" and *participating* by our actions in what God is doing now in our lifetime on earth. . . . In everything we do we are permitted to do his work. What we are aiming for in this vision is to live fully in the kingdom of God and as fully as possible *now* and *here*, not just hereafter. (p. 87)

2. Intention to live in the kingdom as Jesus did:

Jesus makes it possible for us to *intend* to live in the kingdom as he did. We can actually *decide to do it*. Of course that means first of all to trust him, rely on him, to count on him being the Anointed One, the Christ. . . . Concretely, we intend to live in the kingdom of God *by* intending to obey the precise example and teachings of Jesus. This is the form that *trust* in him takes. It does not take the form of merely believing things about him, however true they may be. Indeed, no one can actually believe the truth about him without trusting him by intending to obey him. (p. 87)

3. Means for spiritual transformation:

for the replacing of the inner character of the 'lost' with the inner character of Jesus: his vision, understanding, feelings, decisions, and character. . . . In finding such means we are not left to ourselves but have rich resources available in the teachings of Jesus, in the Scriptures, and in God's people. (p. 89)

Attention is given primarily to the "intention" component of this model as human participation in sanctificational growth is examined. Intention encompasses beliefs accompanied by a "decision to fulfill or carry through with the intention" (p. 88). It is the believer "purposing in his heart" to accomplish something. Thus, intention brings power and order to life processes (p. 88). Intentionality is examined from the aspect of 1) human participation in sanctificational growth in chapter two, 2) free will and belief formation in character development in chapter three, and 3) personal agency beliefs in motivational theory and practice in chapter four.

Sanctification

The notion of personal or spiritual transformation, as most evangelicals perceive it, fits comfortably within an understanding of the doctrine of sanctification. In this section I will provide a brief survey of this doctrine providing a context for a more detailed discussion in the following chapters.

Sanctification Related to Holiness

Sanctification relates to holiness as indicated by the translation of *hagios* in the New Testament. As a noun, it is translated "holy" or "sacred" while as a verb it is translated "make holy, consecrate, or sanctify." *Hagios* also provides the root for "holiness, consecration, and sanctification" *(hagiosmos)* (Seebass, 1976, p. 224). According to theologian Bruce Demarest (1997), "the concept of holiness lies at the heart of the biblical doctrine of sanctification" (p. 406). The following statements support this claim:

1. Sanctification is grounded in the holiness of God (Lev 19:2; Ps 99:5; Isa 5:16).
2. The concept of sanctification in the Old Testament centers on "holiness" and "consecration/separation." Demarest writes that, "the principal OT idea of holiness, then, is cultic and ceremonial. Persons, places, or objects are holy because [they are] separated from what is profane and set apart and devoted to God" (p. 406).
3. The concept of sanctification in the New Testament centers on terms such as "holy," "sacred/ consecrated," and "pure." Demarest states, "In the NT the ceremonial aspect of holiness greatly diminishes. . . . The predominant force of the holiness language in the NT . . . is moral and ethical" (p. 407).

If sanctification is grounded in the holy character of God then the believer's sanctification should demonstrate holiness. If holiness has moral and ethical implications, then the believer's sanctification includes holy conduct. Scripture supports these statements: "As he who called you is holy *[hagion]*, you also be holy *[hagioi]* in all your conduct, since it is written, "You shall be holy *[hagioi]*, for I am holy *[hagios]*." (1 Pet 1:15–16, NEV). These verses imply that a holy God desires a holy people in disposition and conduct. As professor of Religious Studies Stanley Porter (1993) states, "If one must reduce sanctification to a single notion, it may be summarized in the idea that the believer *both* lives in holiness *and* grows into holiness" (p. 399).

Sanctification Related to Christlikeness

Holiness is demonstrated in daily living through Christlikeness as the following theologians claim. New Testament scholar Moises Silva (1988) states that "the standard of holiness is complete conformity to Christ's image (Rom. 8:29)" (p. 1899). Demarest (1997) claims that "holiness, in a word, is Christlikeness daily manifested in the midst of a godless world" (p. 407). Erickson (1985) agrees that "the aim of this divine working is likeness to Christ himself" (p. 970).

Biblically, the connection between progressive holiness or sanctification and Christlikeness is found, according to Demarest (1997, p. 409), in the following passages:

1. 2 Corinthians 3:18; "And we all, with unveiled face, beholding the glory of the Lord, are being transformed into the same image from one degree of glory to another. For this comes from the Lord who is the Spirit."
2. Ephesians 4:15; "Rather, speaking the truth in love, we are to grow up in every way into him who is the head, into Christ".

3. Romans 8:29; "For those whom he foreknew he also predestined to be conformed to the image of his Son, in order that he might be the firstborn among many brothers."
4. Galatians 4:19; "my little children, for whom I am again in the anguish of childbirth until Christ is formed in you!"

Sanctification, therefore, is related to being holy but may also be broadly used to describe the Christian experience of spiritual growth towards Christlikeness.

Progressive Sanctification

Sanctification is a substantive component of the believer's salvation but is distinguished from regeneration, justification, and glorification. According to Demarest, sanctification is the process by which the Christian becomes more like Jesus Christ from the time of regeneration to the time of glorification. He writes that "God who re-creates sinners via a new birth (1Pet 1:3, 23) faithfully renews them into the image of his Son. Sanctification, then, is God's means of actualizing in forgiven sinners his original creative purpose" (p. 385).

Professor of systematic theology Anthony Hoekema (1987) details this renewal process when he writes that it is

> that gracious operation of the Holy Spirit, involving our responsible participation, by which He delivers us as justified sinners from the pollution of sin, renews our entire nature according to the image of God, and enables us to live lives that are pleasing to Him. (p. 61)

Systematic theologian Wayne Grudem's (1994) definition of sanctification parallels Hoekema's: "Sanctification is a progressive work of God and man that makes us more and more free from sin and like Christ in our actual lives" (p. 746). Another systematic theologian Millard Erickson (1985) adds that "sanctification is the continuing work of God in the life of the believer, making him or her actually holy" (i.e., "bearing an actual likeness to God") (pp. 967–968). These definitions emphasize the progressive nature of God's work in making the believer holy.

However, not all theologians agree with this emphasis. David Peterson (1995) believes that definitions emphasizing the progressive nature of sanctification are typical, yet inadequate. He writes that these kinds of definitions obscure "the distinctive meaning and value of the terminology in the New Testament, confusing sanctification with renewal and transformation" (p. 13). Peterson cites Hoekema's definition as an example of those who do not give the definitive aspect of sanctification enough weight. "There is an assumption that sanctification is mainly viewed in *progressive* terms in the New Testament. Little is made of definitive sanctification as a basis and motivation for holy living" (pp. 13–14).

Nevertheless, a comprehensive view of the doctrine of sanctification includes an understanding of both definitive (i.e., positional) and experiential (i.e., progressive) sanctification. Peterson could be criticized for deemphasizing progressive sanctification and as a result supporting a monergistic view of sanctification, that is, God does the work while the believer is passive. I will discuss sanctificational monergism and synergism in chapter two. Again, a more complete understanding of sanctification includes the notion of synergism, that is, believers participate in God's work of sanctification, as will be supported theologically and biblically in this study.

Positional and Progressive Sanctification

The tension between positional and progressive sanctification indicates the need to define these two dimensions of sanctification. Scripture distinguishes two aspects of sanctification. First, positional sanctification, also called objective, judicial, definitive or "the indicative of sanctification" (Demarest, 1997, p. 407), refers to the believer's present status before God as holy – "saints" or "holy ones" (Rom 1:7, Eph 1:1). "We mean the believer's being set aside for God's possession and declared holy by faith in Christ's justifying work" (p. 407). Paul refers to the Corinthians as sanctified even though many of them were acting sinfully (1 Cor 6:11). They had been cleansed of past sins and set apart for God (Lewis and Demarest, 1996, p. 195). Positional sanctification describes the present status of all believers.

Second, progressive sanctification, also called subjective, practical, experiential, or "the imperative of sanctification" (Demarest, 1997, p. 408), refers to the process by which believers, as partakers of God's holiness and empowered by the Spirit of Christ, become more holy and spiritually mature (Heb 6:1, James 1:4). "God's work of effecting Christlikeness in saints is gradual and progressive rather than instantaneous" (Lewis and Demarest, 1996, p. 195). Passages such as 2 Corinthians 3:18, 4:16, 7:1; Ephesians 4:13, 15; and Galatians 4:19 indicate the progressive nature of sanctificational growth.

Though distinguished for clarity, the two dimensions of sanctification should never be separated in theory or practice. As Demarest (1997) states, "[T]he Spirit makes those who are holy in *principle* (i.e., positionally sanctified by grace) holy and godly in *practice* (i.e., experientially sanctified in word and deed)" (p. 385).

This discussion indicates one tension that exists in the doctrine of sanctification. This tension is noted by Silva (1988) as 1) objective-historical vs. subjective-experiential perspectives and 2) judicial vs. transforming aspects. Silva also highlights the "necessity to recognize both the divine agency and human task, the elimination of sin and its suppression, freedom from the law and submission to it, the individual and the corporate concerns, the pessimistic and the optimistic outlooks" when examining sanctification (p. 1902). He attributes the disagreements and perversions of this doctrine to the inability of people to keep these tensions in balance. My goal in chapter two is to ease some of the tension by addressing the "divine agency and human task" issue with an emphasis on need for human participation in progressive sanctification.

Stages of Sanctification

Sanctification is commonly accepted as characterized by three stages, which provide a summary of the doctrine to this point. According to Grudem (1994, pp. 747–750), sanctification can be understood by recognizing the following stages:

    1. Sanctification has a definite beginning at regeneration.

> A definite moral change occurs in our lives at the point of regeneration . . . This initial moral change is the first stage in sanctification. In this sense, there is some overlap between regeneration and sanctification, for this moral change is actually a part of regeneration. But when we view it from the standpoint of moral change within us, we can also see it as the first stage in sanctification. (p. 747)

    Paul sees sanctification as a completed event when he writes, "But you were washed, you were sanctified, you were justified in the name of the Lord Jesus Christ and by the Spirit of our God" (1 Cor 6:11). He also addresses sanctification as beginning at regeneration, "he saved us, not because of works done by us in righteousness, but according to his own mercy, by the washing of regeneration and renewal of the Holy Spirit" (Titus 3:5).

    2. Sanctification increases throughout life.

> Even though the New Testament speaks about a definite beginning to sanctification, it also sees it as a process that continues throughout our Christian lives. This is the primary sense in which sanctification is used in systematic theology and in Christian conversation generally today. . . . All of the moral exhortations and commands in the New Testament epistles apply here, because they all exhort believers to one aspect or another of greater sanctification in their lives. (pp. 748–749)

    Paul writes that Christians "are being changed into the same image [his likeness] from one degree of glory to another" (2 Cor 3:18). The author of Hebrews tells his readers to "lay aside every weight, and sin which clings so closely, and let us run with endurance the race that is set before us" (12:1). These verses and others (Phil 3:9–14; Col 3:10; Heb 12:14; 1 Pt 1:15) also support the notion of progressive sanctification.

    3. Sanctification is completed at death (for our souls) and when the Lord returns (for our bodies).

> Because there is sin that still remains in our hearts even though we have become Christians . . . our sanctification will never be completed in this life. . . . But once we die and go to be with the Lord, then our sanctification is completed in one sense, for our souls are set free from indwelling sin and are made perfect. . . . However, when we appreciate that sanctification involves the whole person, including our bodies . . . then we realize that sanctification will not be entirely completed until the Lord returns and we receive new resurrection bodies. (p. 749) (see Heb 12:23; Rev 21:27; Phil 3:21; 1 Cor 15:23, 49)

From this discussion of positional and progressive sanctification and this brief look at the stages of sanctification, one can conclude that sanctification describes the process of spiritual maturity from the time of regeneration to the time of glorification. Though there are many terms used to describe spiritual growth (e.g., Christian maturity, spiritual transformation, discipleship), they are all referring to sanctification.

Preview of Chapters 2–6

Chapter two argues that believers participate in their sanctificational growth. The chapter examines the claim that human participation is essential in sanctificational growth. Human participation is found in all major evangelical theological traditions and is supported by Scripture though there are some concerns to guard against, which are presented. It is essential that believers, trusting God's resources, make effort in order to grow in sanctification.

If believers are to be involved in the sanctificational process, they must possess the capability to do so. Chapter three examines the believer's capability to intentionally participate in character and sanctificational development. Having examined the theological support for participation (chapter two), I now turn to support from philosophical literature. Free will is examined as it interacts with other components of human nature and character.

In chapter four I introduce a psychological motivational theory into the discussion suggesting coherency in concepts of growth. Sanctificational growth seems to include the component of personal agency beliefs as a motivating factor. Examining Martin Ford's concept of personal agency beliefs provides a basis for discussing the significance of one's perspective of personal capabilities and context to accomplish a goal, both of which seem to be entailed in the theological concept of one's union with Christ.

Chapter five includes a study of sanctificational growth incorporating the concepts that have been examined. First, I compare the theological concept of "union with Christ" with personal agency beliefs to see if there is compatibility. Second, I examine aspects of Romans 6:1–14 to see if there is a fit with Willard's VIM model of personal transformation. The integration of these concepts with an understanding of the believer's union with Christ suggests a conceptual compatibility and may result in a comprehensive understanding of progressive sanctification.

The final chapter presents some educational and ministry implications resulting from this study. The operation of synergism and belief formation in Christian education is briefly examined. Application of the union with Christ concept is made to the individual believer and corporate church. Included are implications for other aspects of church ministry, such as worship and small groups. I conclude with suggestions for further research.

From this brief discussion, it can be observed that sanctification includes the notion that believers participate in God's work of progressive sanctification. This book examines some of the components involved in that participation. I will seek to support the claim that believers have the capability to grow in sanctification while examining what that capability entails.

CHAPTER 2

THE ESSENTIALITY OF
HUMAN PARTICIPATION IN
SANCTIFICATIONAL GROWTH

As seen in chapter one, an issue that is of concern when trying to understand sanctification is the relation between God's role and the believers' role in the progressive aspect of sanctification. Silva (1988) writes, "Much of the controversy focuses on the human role in sanctification. While all Christians agree that holiness would be impossible without God's help, it is difficult to define precisely how that truth affects one's own activity" (p. 1900). The primary claim of this chapter is that believers genuinely participate in sanctificational growth. In other words, progressive sanctification will not take place without the believer's involvement. This claim is made while fully acknowledging the work of God in the process. So, though the believer has a significant responsibility to endeavor to grow spiritually, the effectiveness of that effort is ultimately controlled by a gracious and faithful God who supervises and energizes the believer and the entire process. The interaction of these roles will be referred to as "synergism" in this study.

By examining synergism in sanctification, I will seek to provide an interpretation of the relationship between the Spirit's work and human activity. Thus, while acknowledging the Holy Spirit as the ultimate agent of spiritual formation, the believer acts to effect spiritual growth. Only together can they accomplish what cannot be accomplished separately.

Sanctificational synergism will be argued from two sources. First, I will introduce biblical passages, primarily from Paul's writings, that support sanctificational synergism in forms such as commands to be obeyed, illustrative metaphors, and statements about accountability, along with instructions regarding the work of the Holy Spirit. It is outside the scope of this study to engage in a detailed exegesis of these passages. But, I will use reliable primary and secondary sources to analyze passages so that their support of human participation and synergism in sanctification can be substantiated. Even with limited analysis, evidence of synergism can be seen in Scripture.

Second, I will suggest that sanctificational synergism is supported broadly by all evangelical theologians and traditions regardless of their differing views of sanctification (or salvation). The survey includes Lutheran, Reformed, Dispensational, Keswick, Baptist, Wesleyan, Holiness, and Anglican traditions.

However, among these viewpoints are some who question the role of human participation in sanctification. This may be due to fears that human participation is equal to a "works-righteousness," and thus, contrary to faith and grace. Others may observe that any human effort in sanctification could be considered legalism. Or perhaps they hold a perspective on the sovereignty of God reflective of a view of justification rather than of sanctification. These concerns will be addressed by showing that human participation is a biblical concept and essential for growth in sanctification.

Two explanations of synergism will be proposed. First, I will propose that the divine and human roles are dynamic (not static) in their relationship to one another. Second, I will propose that the divine and human roles act as partners in their relationship to sanctification.

Biblical Support for Human Participation and Synergism in Sanctification

A robust picture of sanctificational synergism may be seen from multiple passages of Scripture. Some texts draw attention to the believer's role (2 Cor 7:1; Heb 12:14) and other texts to God's role (1 Thess 3:11–13; 5:23–24) in progressive sanctification. A few passages include both (Phil 2:12–13; Col 1:29; 2 Pet 1:3–8). I will focus on two key passages that demonstrate the necessity of human participation in progressive sanctification. Next, biblical evidence for synergism is presented by examining two metaphors indicating human participation. The believer's future accountability, which also supports human participation, is then introduced. Since sanctificational synergism involves the work of God through the Spirit, this divine aspect of God's work completes the portrayal of progressive sanctification. In the following discussion, human participation is presented as an aspect of synergism in sanctification. However, the two concepts may be used interchangeably in the discussion.

Analysis of Key Biblical Passages

Strong biblical support for human participation in sanctification lies in the numerous testimonial statements of the Apostle Paul and in the commands of Scripture that believers have the responsibility to obey. Theologian John Walvoord (1987) claims that "many exhortations of Scripture become meaningless if there is not some human responsibility associated with these aspects of salvation" (p. 224). By relating the example of Paul and the need to obey biblical commands with the progressive aspect of sanctification, the necessity of human effort will be evident.

Pauline Passages

The Apostle Paul offers an explicit portrayal of synergism related to sanctification. First, he records his own attestation of a dynamic interaction between his work and God's work in his life and ministry.

> But by the grace of God I am what I am, and his grace toward me was not in vain. On the contrary, I worked harder than any of them, though it was not I, but the   grace of God that is with me. (1 Corinthians 15:10)

> For this I toil, struggling with all his energy that he powerfully works within me. (Colossians 1:29)

> For we know, brothers loved by God, that he has chosen you, because our gospel came to you not only in word, but also in power and in the Holy Spirit and with full conviction. You know what kind of men we proved to be among you for your sake. (1 Thessalonians 1:4–5)

Second, he also provides statements referring to effective Christian living that indicate synergism.

> For the grace of God has appeared, bringing salvation for all people, training us to renounce ungodliness and worldly passions, and to live self-controlled, upright, and godly lives in the present age. (Titus 2:11–12)

> If we live by the Spirit, let us also walk by the Spirit. (Galatians 5:25)

I have chosen two Scripture passages that represent sanctificational synergism for more detailed examination. The first passage demonstrates the necessity for believers to participate in their sanctification and the second passage presents a robust picture of synergism.

1 Thessalonians 4:3–4, 7

Paul's visit to Thessalonica on his second missionary journey, though successful in the conversion of Jews and Greeks (Acts 17:1–4), ended abruptly when threatened by a mob stirred by jealous Jews (Acts 17:5–10). Without adequate instruction and leadership, this new church faced the same kind of persecution experienced by Paul and his companions (Green, 2002, p. 51). Paul, deeply concerned about the spiritual condition of this floundering church, sent Timothy to encourage them and determine the status of their faith (1 Thess 2:17–3:5). Timothy brought back a glowing report of their steadfastness in the faith but also informed Paul of issues that were lacking in their faith (3:6–10). So, in this letter, Paul instructed these young converts regarding belief and conduct so that they would faithfully continue in their relationship with God and in their own spiritual growth (5:23–24). This included instruction regarding sanctification (3:10–13; 4:3–7; 5:23–24).

Paul prayed that God would establish these young converts in holiness (3:10–13) and sanctify them wholly (5:23–24). In his concluding prayer, Paul spoke of sanctification as the work of God, "Now may the God of peace himself sanctify you completely, and may your whole spirit, soul, and body be kept blameless at the coming of our Lord Jesus Christ. He who called you is faithful; he will surely do it" (5:23–24). Paul confidently states his belief that sanctification is clearly a work of God wrought in the believer's heart, mind, and body.

But, between these two references to God's work of holiness or sanctification, Paul speaks of sanctification as God's strategy in which believers participate. He uses language indicating that believers have a responsibility in his plan of sanctification. "For this is the will of God, your sanctification [*hagiosmos*]: that you abstain from sexual immorality . . . control [your] own body in holiness [*hagiosmo*] and honor . . . For God has not called us for impurity, but in holiness [*hagiosmo*]" (1 Thess. 4:3–4, 7).

Paul had been instructing the church at Thessalonica how they "ought to live and to please God" (4:1) with an urgency that they continue to follow his directives (i.e., "do so more and more"). The instructions on living and pleasing God, given to them "through the Lord Jesus" (4:2) included further injunctions regarding the will of God, which Paul now revealed to these believers. Though all of Paul's instruction may be acknowledged as the will of God, he specifically classifies this statement regarding sanctification as "the will of God," that is, "God's moral plan for human beings that should be both known and put into practice" (Green, 2002, p. 189–190).

Since the text reads, "For this is the will of God, your sanctification," there is some debate concerning the nature of God's will here. Is the "will of God" a divine decree such that sanctification is inevitable or an indication of God's moral will in which believers must participate? The context provides the best evidence to help our understanding. Paul is addressing "brothers" and giving instruction based on being "in the Lord Jesus" (v. 1) eliminating the idea that God's will here refers to his "saving will" (Gal 1:4, Eph 1:5, 9). Nor does it refer to God's "sovereign will"—"God's secret plan that determines everything in the universe" (Friesen, 1980, pp. 32–33)—since this will has already been revealed for all to see and know. The context indicates that God's will here refers to his moral will for the believer since Paul's instructions involve how to live and what to do (v. 1).

Additionally, Best (1972) and Frame (1988) agree that the kind of sanctification referred to as God's will is not passive but "reflexive," (i.e., "that you may sanctify yourselves") since the emphasis of the passage is on what they are to do. Doing this kind of active will contrasts with being carried along passively by "the passion of lust like the Gentiles" (v. 5) (Green, 2002, p. 189).

However, Morris (1991) regards this sanctification here as a gift and a demand (p. 119). Though sanctification is a gift given at regeneration, that kind of sanctification does not seem to be the emphasis in this passage. Here it seems Paul emphasizes the progressive nature of sanctification since he urges the Thessalonians to action. In fact, he describes sanctification as avoiding sexual immorality. In the context of instruction regarding their conduct, they are urged to live a sanctified life which means they are to participate in their sanctification. Participation is explicitly suggested by the text as these believers are urged to "align their conduct with the will of God" (Green, 2002, p. 190).

The emphasis on human action, however, does not diminish the need for divine participation also noted in this context. God has called believers to sanctification (v. 7) and this is not to be disregarded since God provides "his Holy Spirit" that every believer might fulfill this calling (v. 8). Therefore, the progressive sanctification of the Thessalonian believers, which can be applied to all believers, seems to be God's principal concern. Though there are other aspects to God's will (5:18), here the emphasis is on God's will concerning sanctification which directly links to their sexual conduct.

What aspects regarding sanctification are these believers to know and practice? By what means are believers to carry out God's will regarding sanctification? The verbs in the passage help answer the question. First, believers are to "abstain" from sexual immorality (v.4). Second, believers are to "know" how to control their body (i.e., "possess their own body" (Green, 2002, p. 194; Morris, 1991, p. 120) or "keep his wife" (Best, 1972, p. 158)) in holiness and honor (v. 5). Third, believers are not to "transgress and wrong/defraud/take advantage of" other believers in "sexual" matters (Green, 2002, p. 197; Morris, 1991, p. 124; Best, 1972, p.167) (v.6). There seems to be strong indication that God's will regarding one aspect of sanctification is that the believer's life be characterized by a separation from the sinful practice of sexual immorality (Wanamaker, 1990, p. 150) and commitment to moral goodness.

It seems evident that the kind of sanctification practiced by keeping oneself sexually upright is the responsibility of every believer. Though it is God's will that believers live like this, he does not produce sexual morality in their lives. It is believers who engage in chaste living in cooperation with the Holy Spirit (Gal 5:22–23). They must participate by obediently carrying out God's will for sanctification.

Philippians 2:12–13

A frequently cited passage indicating synergism is Philippians 2:12–13: "Therefore, my beloved, as you have always obeyed, so now, not only as in my presence but much more in my absence, work out your own salvation with fear and trembling, for it is God who works in you, both to will and to work for his good pleasure."

Paul has addressed an aspect of obedience in this passage by urging an application of Christ's example (v. 8) by the Philippians themselves, both while Paul was with them and currently in his absence (cf. 1:27). This obedience was in some way related to their "salvation" which they received "from God" (1:28). The imperative "work out your own salvation" has created difficulties in the understanding of Paul's message. Though it is outside the scope of this discussion to engage in a detailed analysis of these verses, this phrase must be explained to understand its contribution to the notion of synergism suggested here.

The biblical idea of "salvation" (*soteria*) or "save" (*sozo*) is multi-faceted in meaning. Its basic meaning is "deliverance" whereby a person is rescued from some danger; as in healing a person from illness (Mk 5:28), from enemies (Ps 44:7), or from the possibility of death (Mt 8:25). However, there is a positive facet to "salvation" resulting in a state of well-being or wholeness (Mt 5:28, 34;

Acts 4:9; 2 Tim 4:18) (Marshall, 1988, p. 610). In New Testament theology the word "becomes a technical term describing God's action in rescuing people from their sins and their consequences and in bringing them into a situation where they experience his blessings" (Marshall, 1988, p. 610; see also Walters and Milne, 1996, pp. 1046-1050; Schneider, 1978, pp. 205–216). There is also a sense of "preservation" (i.e., "keep from harm") to the term (Mk 13:20; Lk 9:24; Acts 27:20, 28). At the least, Paul uses the noun *soteria* to refer to spiritual or eschatological salvation (Phil 1:19, 28; 2:13) (Schneider and Caneday, p. 184).

It seems, therefore, that salvation has two initial and unending consequences. First, there is deliverance from sin and guilt (Rom 5:1; Heb 10:22). Second, there is the placement into wholeness or the benefits of God (Eph 1:3). "Salvation is then understood comprehensively as the sum-total of the benefits bestowed on believers by God (Lk 19:9; Rom 1:16)" (Marshall, 1988, p. 610).

It is clear from Scripture that sinners are unable to deliver themselves from their own sin (Eph. 2: 8, 9; Titus 3:4–7). Therefore, God has mercifully intervened to save sinners in the person of Jesus Christ (Rom 4:25; 5:10; 2 Cor 4:10f.; Phil 2:6f.; 1 Tim 1:15; 1 John 4:9–10, 14) through his death and resurrection (1 Cor 15:5f) and by the blood of his cross (Acts 20:28; Rom 3:25; 5:9; Eph 1:7; Col 1:20; Heb 9:12; 1 John 1:7). People are invited to hear and respond in faith to God's salvation in this gospel message (Rom 10:8, 14f; 1 Cor 1:18–25; 15:11; 1 Thess 1:4f) (Walters and Milne, 1996, p. 1050).

Thus, in Philippians 2:12, when believers are urged to "work out" their salvation, it seems that the work must in some way differ from a self-deliverance from sin. However, it may relate to experiencing the blessings and benefits of salvation. In other words, believers work to accomplish a greater experience of God's benefits which they already posses.

In the New Testament, there are passages that indicate that salvation has been accomplished and is the present possession of the believer (Eph 2:5, 8; Titus 3:5; 2 Tim 1:9; Rom 8:24). But New Testament writers often describe salvation as something that will occur in the future (Matt 10:22; 24:13; Rom 5:9–10; 1 Thess 5:8-9; Heb 9:28; 1 Pet 1:4–5) (Schreiner and Caneday, 2001, pp. 48–52). Associating these two aspects of salvation suggests that there is an "already/not yet" connotation related to this term that may find expression in Paul's use of the term in Philippians 2:12. The notion that salvation is possessed by believers presently and yet must continually be "worked out" for future fulfillment, may also fit Paul's instruction here and provide an explanation for this difficult statement.

To understand this phrase, we must also decipher the meaning of "work out." *Katergazesthe*, translated "work out" in Philippians 2:12 is also translated "achieve" or "accomplish" (Rom 1:27; 7:15, 17f, 20; 1 Cor 5:3; 1 Pet 4:3) and "bring about," "produce," or "create" (Rom 4:15; 5:3; 7:8, 13; 2 Cor 7:10f; 9:11) (Gingrich, 1983, p. 105). Rogers and Rogers (1998) state that the verb means "to work out, to work on to the finish. The Prep[osition] in compound is perfective and views the linear progress down to the goal: 'work on to the finish'" (p. 452). When related to salvation, it might translate: "achieve/accomplish your salvation," bring your salvation to completion," "work on your salvation to the finish."

Paul seems to be urging the Philippians and all believers to obedience by "bringing their salvation to completion." In other words, believers are to diligently participate in the "not yet" aspect of salvation once they are "saved." It could also mean that believers are to labor diligently and intentionally in order to experience the benefits of God's salvific blessings until salvation is fully completed. This understanding of "work out" does strongly support the human participation aspect of sanctificational synergism. Believers are to participate in bringing their salvation to completion.

Greek professor Gerald Hawthorne (1983) provides a contrasting explanation of this phrase. He claims that the exhortation to "work out your own salvation" is not aimed at individuals but to the whole church together as a community so that their "work" has to do with the spiritual well-being of the church (p. 98-99). Thus, he translates this phrase, "Obediently work at achieving spiritual health" (p. 96). "Salvation," then, is reduced to "spiritual health" or wholeness in the church and what they "work out" is changed to what they "work at." *Soteria* ("salvation") may be translated "strength" (ESV) or "health" in Acts 27:34 and *sozo* ("save") can mean "whole" (Matt 9:21–22; Mark 6:56; 10:52) or "healed" (Matt 5:23) as deliverance from disease. However, it normally refers to "spiritual or eschatological salvation" (Phil 1:19, 28) particularly in Paul's writing (Schreiner and Caneday, p. 184). Hawthorne seems to weaken Paul's exhortation by limiting these believers' work to their church's health.

The Philippians are to "bring their salvation to completion" as individuals, but this work is to be accomplished in the context of the community of believers (see O'Brien, 1991, p. 279–280). Paul may be addressing both individuals and the corporate body. New Testament scholar Gordon Fee (1995) supports this view.

> What Paul is referring to, therefore, is the *present* "outworking" of their *eschatological salvation* within the *believing community* in Philippi. At issue is obedience," pure and simple, which in this case is defined as their "working or car-rying out in their corporate life the salvation that God has graciously given hem." (p. 235).

Two arguments can be used to fend off accusations that this interpretation advocates a "works" salvation. First, Paul urges the Philippians to "work out their salvation" with "fear and trembling" which "indicates a nervous and trembling anxiety to do right" (Rogers and Rogers, 1998, p. 452) or "human vulnerability" (Fee, p. 236) and humble recognition of weakness. This seems antithetical to those who trust their own ability, are self-sufficient and self-reliant regarding their own salvation.

Second, this work related to salvation is only possible because it is God's work. Paul continues to explain obedience as possible because "it is God who works in you, both to will and to work for his good pleasure" (v. 13). The verse begins with God (*Theos*) indicating that he is the principal agent to bring this work of salvation to completion. Paul "immediately places the imperative within the context of God's prior action" (Fee, p. 237).

What is God's work (*energōn*) here? Danker (2002) indicates that this use of the term "work" denotes a "transitive" work that "produces" or has "effect" on something or someone; meaning "to bring something about through the use of capability" (p. 335). (1 Cor 12:6— "who empowers them all;" Eph 1:11— "works all things;" 2:2— "the spirit that is now at work in the sons of disobedience") (p. 66). God himself is powerfully active in effecting his will through the abilities of his people. Fee (1995) explains its use in this context: "This verb, as elsewhere, does not mean that God is 'doing it for them,' but that God supplies the necessary empowering. . . . [T]heir obedience is ultimately something that God effects in/among them" for his own good pleasure (pp. 237–238).

What does God do as he works in the believer? Paul writes that God works "both to will and to work for his good pleasure" (v. 13b). God causes the "willing" and the "working" to obey as believers determine and work to obey. There seems to be a dynamic interaction of God's will and the believer's will and of God's work and the believer's work that plays out from conversion to final salvation probably through the power of the Holy Spirit. "God energises your will and your activity in order that you may fulfil his good pleasure in your completed salvation" (Vincent, 1897, p. 67).

The point of this discussion is to demonstrate that Philippians 2:12–13 supports synergism in progressive sanctification. Paul urges the Philippians to obedience because God empowers them to do the work of completing their salvation bringing him great pleasure. It has not been necessary to look at every detail of this passage to conclude that both God and the believer have a significant role in the Christian's spiritual development. God's work is prioritized, but the believer's obedience is not minimized (Schreiner and Caneday, 2001, p. 185).

In attempting to delimit what is meant here, we could say that these verses state that God is not doing the work for believers (i.e., they are not passive) nor is his will overpowering them (i.e., their will is not lost in his). They can will to do and actually achieve God's good pleasure in an ongoing work but only as God works in them.

It is outside the scope of this study to reach a definitive conclusion on the interpretation of this text. This exercise simply suggests that my view is compatible with the major interpretations presented. My purpose is to demonstrate the reality of the divine-human co-operation (synergism) in spiritual growth. Philippians 2:12–13 indicates that both God and believers are at work as partners or co-workers; believers enabled by the Holy Spirit to live out a growing obedience to Jesus Christ. Theologian John Murray (1962) summarizes this passage.

> Our working is not dispensed with or made superfluous because God works; God's working is not suspended because we work. There is the correlation and conjunction of both. The fact that God works in us is the encouragement and incentive to our working. Indeed, God's working is the energizing cause of our working both in willing and doing. Our working is the index to God's working; if we do not work, the working of God is absent. Presumptuous self-confidence

is excluded…the more assured we are that God works in us, the more diligent and persistent we are in our working. Our whole personality is not only drawn within the scope of but also enlisted in all its functions in that process that moves to the goal of being conformed to the image of God's Son. (pp. 232–233)

This passage illustrates the active role of believers in sanctificational growth. On one hand believers are actively depending upon God to sanctify them. On the other hand, believers are actively striving to obey God and are intentionally taking steps to increase their sanctification.

The Pauline passages noted in this discussion provide a strong support for human participation in progressive sanctification. Believers are responsible to understand and obey the commands of Scripture in order for sanctification to be experientially realized.

Pauline Metaphors

Human participation in progressive sanctification is evident in the metaphors Paul uses to describe aspects of the Christian life. In this section I will examine two examples. Silva (1988) states that "Sanctification requires discipline, concentration, and effort, as is clear by the many exhortations of Scripture, especially those where the Christian life is described with such figures as running and fighting" (p. 1900). Paul describes Christian living as "running" and "boxing" in 1 Corinthians 9:24–27 and as "fighting" in Ephesians 6:10–17.

1 Corinthians 9:24–27

The Apostle Paul, illustrating his own methodology for effective witness (9:19–23), uses athletic metaphors to describe significant aspects of Christian living.

Do you not know that in a race all the runners compete, but only one receives the prize? So run that you may obtain it. Every athlete exercises self-control in all things. They do it to receive a perishable wreath, but we an imperishable. So I do not run aimlessly; I do not box as one beating the air. But I discipline my body and keep it under control, lest after preaching to others I myself should be disqualified. (1 Cor 9:24–27)

The idea that running involves strenuous effort is in the basic meaning of the term. According to Arndt and Gingrich (1979) "running," used figuratively here, means to "exert oneself to the limit of one's powers in an attempt to go forward" or "strive to advance" (p. 825). It is striving purposefully for the goal with all one's strength just as the one who wins the prize does. Such effort certainly entails discipline and training if one is to "get the prize" or harm may come while exerting one's self fully when not properly prepared. Barrett states, "The Christian must not only start but continue in the right way; it is implied that he must put forth all his strength. The process also implies self-discipline"

(p. 217). Disciplined effort prepares and sustains believers toward the desired result.

The same is true for "boxing." Self-discipline and focused determination are the opposite of "beating the air" which may signify "the failure of the pugilist to make his blows count or his carrying on [a] mock contest as a shadow boxer" (Rogers and Rogers, 1998, p. 370), neither of which qualify one to win a prize. A properly fought boxing match involves a disciplined and controlled body.

Believers are to obey the imperative to "run that you may obtain [the prize]." This involves disciplined, self-controlled, but strenuous effort on their part. This metaphor seems to strongly support human participation in sanctificational growth.

Ephesians 6:10–17

In Ephesians 6:10–17, Paul urges his readers to "put on the full armor of God" that they might be "strong in the Lord and in the strength of his might" (v. 11). Immediately we notice a synergism implied in this passage. Believers must put on the armor but when they do, it is the strength of the Lord that they experience.

To wage the battle against the "schemes of the devil" (v. 11, 16) and other spiritual forces (v. 12) while standing firm "in the evil day," believers are commanded to action. Therefore, they are to "take up the whole armor of God" (v. 13), with "the belt of truth," the "breastplate of righteousness" (v. 14), and the shoes of "readiness" in place (v. 15). Additionally, they are to take up the "shield of faith" (v. 16), the "helmet of salvation," and the "sword of the Spirit" (v. 17) while continually praying and staying alert (v. 18). Many of these actions are imperatives which must be obeyed. There is effort involved in standing firm against evil forces.

Preparations begin by "putting on the armor." Arndt and Gingrich (1979) define this middle voice term as "clothe oneself in, put on, wear something" (p. 264). As one would put on clothes, one is to put on this armor. It is an imperative that "might well suggest a sense of urgency incumbent on the believers. The middle voice indicates that they are responsible for putting on the full armor" (Hoehner, 2002, p. 822).

Paul is concerned that believers wear the protection provided by God so they can "be strong in the Lord" in the midst of the spiritual battle. The believer has the responsibility to take the armor and put it on. In obedience to this command, there is activity and effort. It is by clothing oneself in God's armor, that is, the resources God provides, that one is able to withstand Satan's attacks and thus, persevere. Human participation and synergism are seen as Christians "put on" what God supplies resulting in strength to endure.

Accountability

Sometime in the future, believers will give account before God (2 Cor 5:10). For what will God hold them accountable? Scripture, most notably in 1 Corinthians 3:10–15 teaches that believers will give account to God for their "work." Paul teaches that a day is coming when "everyone's work will be exposed and seen from the divine perspective" (Fee, 1987, p. 141). There seems to be a relationship between the resultant efforts of building something and the work that is examined. Gingrich (1983) defines *ergon* here "in the passive sense, indicating what is produced by work" (p. 77). It is the same term used to describe the golden calf made by rebellious Israel (Acts 7:41), God's creation (Heb 1:10), creations of humankind (2 Pet 3:10), and Satan's work (1 John 3:8). Perhaps "workmanship" would be a proper synonym since the quality of what is produced by the work is implied here.

What affects the quality of the work? In the context, Paul mentioned a "fleshly" ("merely human" v. 4) ministry that leads to division among the church (3:1–4) contrasted with a united ministry that labors in cooperation with God (3:5–9). A quality work is built on the foundation of Jesus Christ (3:11, 14) and is built by those who work in the Holy Spirit (3:16–17). In other words, quality work may be characterized by synergism. It is a work produced by those who acknowledge they are co-workers with God (3:9).

Thus, the believers' efforts of a lifetime, that is their workmanship, will be revealed by fire that tests the quality of their work. Those building with

> "gold, silver, and costly stones," will see their work "survive" the test, and they "will receive their reward." On the other hand, those who persist in pursuing *sophia* [wisdom apart from God], who are building with "wood, hay, or straw," will see their work consumed and they themselves "will suffer loss"—although their loss, [Paul] is quick to qualify, does not refer to their salvation. (Fee, 1987, p. 142–143)

This passage seems to teach that believers, who are held accountable by God for what they have done, are therefore responsible to erect an enduring building on the foundation of Jesus Christ. Human participation is necessary. The one who builds such a structure is enabled by the Holy Spirit (3:16–17) which is another indication of synergism.

The Role of the Holy Spirit in Sanctification

Though believers are responsible to participate in the sanctification process, sanctification is not possible apart from the Holy Spirit. Moreover, a sanctified life is inconceivable apart from the Holy Spirit (Rom 15:16; 2 Thess 2:13; 1 Pet 1:2; and cf. 1 Cor 6:11) (Brower, 1996, p. 1059). New Testament scholar Donald Guthrie (1981) writes that "the standard of sanctification is a holiness acceptable to God, that is, a holiness in line with the Spirit's own character. The process of making holy is, therefore, peculiarly characteristic of the Spirit's activities" (p. 554).

The insights gleaned from the following passages show the significance of the Holy Spirit's work in sanctification. The first three passages indicate the Spirit's work in the initial phase or "state" of sanctification known as "positional sanctification."

Paul records in Romans 15:15b–16 that he has written his letter "because of the grace given me by God to be a minister of Christ Jesus to the Gentiles in the priestly service of the gospel of God, so that the offering of the Gentiles may be acceptable, sanctified by the Holy Spirit." According to Fee (1994), Paul writes as Christ's priestly servant, who presents his "offering" of the Gentiles who have been "sanctified by the Holy Spirit" so that the Jews might accept them. The "offering" is most likely the Gentiles themselves (Moo, 1996, p. 890). Those who had been formerly unclean have now been purified and consecrated by the Holy Spirit probably at the time of their conversion. Here, the perfect passive participle form of sanctify is used by Paul and could be translated "having been sanctified." This is accomplished "by the Spirit." In this setting, knowing that Paul's ministry has nothing to do with the sacrificial system, the "consecration" or "sanctification" of this offering of Gentile believers means that they are "set apart for God's own holy purposes. And this in turn always for Paul carries with it the connotation of godliness, including godly behavior" (Fee, 1994, p. 627). The Spirit is holy and by his presence makes even Gentile believers holy.

In 2 Thessalonians 2:13, "to be saved through the sanctifying work of the Spirit," is understood as an indication of the whole person being sanctified by the Holy Spirit thus making the whole person holy. (Morris, 1991, p. 239; Wanamaker, 1990; Green, 2002). According to this statement, sanctification relates to salvation, as is true in other passages (1 Cor 6:11; 2 Cor 1:21–22; Gal 4:4–6). "Far from being auxiliary to their salvation, the apostle understands the *sanctifying work* as the action *of the Spirit of* God that brings about salvation" (Green, 2002, p. 327). The Holy Spirit plays a central in this work of sanctification.

Election in 1 Peter 1:1–2 is explained as effectual by means of "the sanctification of the Spirit." J. N. D. Kelly (1969), early church specialist, believes Peter is referring to the means of "predestinating choice" made operative by the action of the Holy Spirit who is the agent of cleansing and consecration (p. 43). These verses indicate a connection between election (v. 1), foreknowledge (v. 2), and sanctification in the Spirit, all of which are divine acts. The Spirit is central to conversion itself (Fee, 1994, p. 876) He is the agent of this initial salvific work of sanctification.

Not only is the Holy Spirit the agent of sanctification initially, he is also the agent of sanctification continuously. The Holy Spirit is central to progressive sanctification as the following verses indicate.

And we all, with unveiled face, beholding the glory of the Lord, are being transformed into the same image from one degree of glory to another. For this come from he Lord who is the Spirit. (2 Cor 3:18)

But I say, walk by the Spirit, and you will not gratify the desires of the flesh. . . . If we live by the Spirit, let us also walk by the Spirit. (Gal 5:16–25)

[T]hat according to the riches of his glory he may grant you to be strengthened with power through his Spirit in your inner being, so that Christ may dwell in your hearts through faith. (Eph 3:14–17a)

[H]e saved us, not because of works done by us in righteousness, but according to his own mercy, by the washing of regeneration and renewal of the Holy Spirit, whom he poured out on us richly through Jesus Christ our Savior, so that being justified by his grace we might become heirs according to the hope of eternal life. (Titus 3:5–7)

These verses seem to indicate that sanctification or holiness, practiced as "walking by means of the Holy Spirit" is "two-dimensional." First, it means abstaining from certain sins—absolutely—by "serving God 'in the newness of the Spirit' (Rom 7:6)" and by putting to death "the former way of life (Rom 6:1–18; 8:12–13; Col 3:5–11)." Second, it also means that the Holy Spirit lives in believers, "reproducing the life of Christ within/among them, especially in their communal relationships." (Fee, 1994, p. 881).

Thus, sanctification, both positional and progressive, is conceivable only by the work of the Holy Spirit. He is in the saving event by which believers are made "the sanctified" (i.e., holy ones or saints) as well as in the ongoing work of living in harmony with their holy state.

However, though the Holy Spirit operates in both positional and progressive sanctification, the believer is made holy (i.e., positional sanctification) apart from any effort yet co-operates with the Holy Spirit in progressive sanctification. This will become clearer as this study continues.

Scripture supports human participation and synergism in progressive sanctification. It pictures synergism in metaphor and in explanations of future accountability. It also indicates that the Holy Spirit is the dynamic agent of both aspects of sanctification (viz., positional and progressive) providing the key to understanding the divine-human interaction in synergism. Along with biblical support for human participation and synergism in sanctification, there is also theological support.

Theological Support for Human Participation in Sanctification

The literature from conservative evangelicalism generally supports the notion of human participation at some level in sanctificational growth. Each viewpoint highlighted in the two works, *Five Views of Sanctification* (Gundry, 1987) and *Christian Spirituality* (Alexander, 1988), indicates human involvement in sanctification. In this section, the evidence supporting human participation is presented from a theological perspective.

Views of Contemporary Evangelical Systematic Theologians

Most evangelical theologians support the idea of human participation being essential to growth in sanctification. A few examples are presented here.

Millard Erickson (1985) writes, "While sanctification is exclusively of God, that is, its power rests entirely on his holiness, the believer is constantly exhorted to work and to grow in the matters pertaining to salvation" (p. 971). Bruce Demarest (1997) agrees, "Sanctification involves both God's provision and the Christian's participation. . . . Although the initiative in sanctification is with God, necessary also are the believer's willing and working" (p. 402). Wayne Grudem (1994) also agrees:

> God works in our sanctification and we work as well, and we work for the same purpose. We are not saying that we have equal roles in sanctification or that we both work in the same way, but simply that we cooperate with God in ways that are appropriate to our status as God's creatures. (p. 753)

Gordon Lewis and Bruce Demarest (1996) state, "Although the Holy Spirit is its [the spiritual life's] ultimate causal agent, he is not the only causal agent. Christians are ontologically real agents who actively work together with the Spirit" (vol. 3, p. 214).

Thomas Oden (1994) makes a clear statement about sanctifying grace as it works in the individual believer who is responsible to work as well.

> It is characteristic of the Holy Spirit to work personally and uniquely in each recipient to do what is proportionally and contextually required and salutary to draw that person closer to God. If this were not so, then there would be nothing to do after receiving God's pardon, no works of love in response to grace, only quiet receptive passivity that does not cooperate or cowork. Growth in grace does not occur through quiescent inactivism or simply doing nothing. (p. 221)

To the views of these evangelical theologians, I now add the weight of evidence from various orthodox theological traditions. All point toward a belief that believers have a part in progressive sanctification.

By reviewing the literature of each theological tradition, I will demonstrate that human participation in sanctification is commonly accepted among the traditions, though the individual traditions may indicate differing views of how that participation works. The concept of divine-human co-operation is present to some degree in every tradition though the term synergism is rarely used. For purposes of this discussion, the terms will be used interchangeably.

Lutheran View

Gerhard Forde (1988), professor of theology and Lutheran scholar, states that sanctification is "the art of getting used to justification" (p. 13) or consists in being "shaped" by justification (p. 23). Apparently, this artistry and shaping includes God who produces sanctification and Christians who in some sense cooperate in the production. However, a key tenet of the Lutheran view of sanctification is that cooperation must not ignore grace. Forde continues to explain:

> There is a kind of growth and progress, it is to be hoped, but it is growth in grace—a growth in coming to be captivated more and more, if we can so speak, by the totality, the unconditionality of the grace of God. (p. 27)

Lutheran theologian Francis Pieper (1953) advocates a weightier role to human activity. Pieper answers the question, "Who effects sanctification?" by stating that the Christian "plays an active role; he co-operates." However, he is emphatic that the working of God and the working of believers are not "coordinate" but that the believer's activity is always "fully subordinated" to God's activity through the ministry of the Holy Spirit (p. 14).

Taking both of these statements into consideration, it seems that the Lutheran position seeks to diligently guard against any kind of human effort apart from God's grace infusing the effort, while acknowledging some level of human participation. This view is similar to the Reformed view.

Reformed View

In the Reformed view sanctification is "both a grace and a duty" (Shedd, 1888, p. 555–556). Thus, sanctificational synergism is commonly described as the believer *cooperating* with God (Hodge, 1946, p. 215; Shedd, 2003, p. 804; Kuyper, 1900, p. 488). Louis Berkof (1933) represents this view.

> God and not man is the author of sanctification. This does not mean, however, that man is entirely passive in the process. He can and should co-operate with God in the work of sanctification by a diligent use of the means which God has placed at his disposal. (p. 267)

Sinclair Ferguson (1988) expands this viewpoint:

> God gives increase in holiness by engaging our minds, wills, emotions and actions. We are involved in the process. That is why biblical teaching on sanctification appears in both the indicative ("I the Lord sanctify you") and the imperative ("sanctify yourselves this day") (p. 67).

It seems clear that the Reformed view supports sanctificational synergism with its inclusion of human participation in the sanctificational process.

Dispensational View

The Dispensational view firmly upholds sanctificational synergism and emphasizes human responsibility and activity in the process of sanctification according to Ryrie (1982, p. 191). Lewis Sperry Chafer (1948) emphasizes the progressive nature of Christian growth. He writes, "the knowledge of truth, devotion, and the Christian experience are naturally subject to development . . .

That development should be advanced with each passing day" (p. 285). The believer is responsible for the development of knowledge, truth, and devotion but not exclusive of God's grace.

John Walvoord (1987) provides a clear description of sanctificational synergism according to this tradition.

> Dispensationalists, while usually Calvinistic, object to making conversion and sanctification wholly the sovereign acts of God apart from human participation. Though agreeing that both conversion and sanctification flow from the grace of God and that it is impossible for people to accomplish either one by themselves, dispensationalists hold that the many exhortations of Scripture become meaningless if there is not some human responsibility associated with these aspects of salvation. . . . The truth is that God has sovereignly given human beings a will that, in the case of Christians, has been supernaturally and graciously enabled to make choices. . . . The Scriptures are just as clear that people are responsible for responding to the truth of God and to the work of the Holy Spirit, which permits God to work out His program of sanctification. . . . [S]anctification is the work of God in the heart of the individual. It is accomplished only in harmony with the human response. (pp. 224–225)

Keswick or Victorious Life View

The Keswick view holds that the believer must decisively surrender to God in a crisis event but will also cooperate with God to progress in sanctification. "God works sanctification in the believer to the extent that the latter ceases to strive and permits the Lord to do it all" (Demarest, 1997, p. 397). The Keswick movement is not a denomination or doctrinal system but it does have a distinctive view of sanctification. Its distinction lies in the view that the victorious Christian life includes a necessary crisis event of total surrender in the process of sanctification. This event differs from the "entire sanctification" of Wesleyans since, in the Keswick view, sin is not fully removed.

The Keswick perspective recognizes the need for a balanced solution to the emphases between divine and human roles in sanctification. Their solution is to emphasize the action by the believer of full surrender to the Holy Spirit who then produces holiness in the surrendered one's life. In this process, according to McQuilkin (1987),

> God does influence our minds directly, but His primary method of bringing about growth is through what are commonly called 'means of grace,' or conduits of divine energy. In these means we are not passive but must participate actively. Even though God indeed works in us both the willing and doing of His good pleasure, we are to work out our own salvation with fear and trembling (p. 180).

The means of grace are prayer, Scripture, church, and suffering. Though available to all, not all take advantage of these "tools of the Spirit." To grow in sanctification, believers must avail themselves of these means through which

God works towards growth. This seems to be the extent of human involvement necessary in the Keswick perspective once surrender has taken place.

Baptist View

Baptists commonly view sanctification as brought about by the grace of God through faith including some level of human activity. Acknowledging that sanctification is the work of the triune God and that its pattern in the New Testament is passive, James Garrett (1995), a Baptist theologian, writes:

> Sanctification is by the grace of God through faith. Human beings cannot be made holy in any perfected sense without their voluntary or active participation. God is not the sanctifier of robots but of human creatures. . . . Although sanctification is not synonymous with "moral improvement," it does call for "active obedience." (p. 368)

In his classic *Systematic Theology*, Baptist theologian A. A. Strong (1907) upholds a Reformed view that emphasizes the Christian's participation as primarily involved in mortifying the flesh and in obedience.

> The operation of God [in sanctification] reveals itself in, and is accompanied by, intelligent and voluntary activity of the believer in the discovery and mortification of sinful desires, and in the bringing of the whole being into obedience to Christ and conformity to the standards of his word. (p. 871)

Wesleyan View

In the Wesleyan view, sanctification, the beginning of holiness, begins at the new birth or regeneration. Though there is some progress made in sanctification from this inception of holiness, much emphasis is placed on a distinct event taking place for true sanctification. (Due to the strong emphasis on "entire sanctification" in Wesleyanism, it is mentioned here so it can be examined but only as it relates to human participation.) This concept is described as "entire sanctification" and is defined as

> the act of God by which the human heart is cleansed from all sin and filled with love by the Holy Spirit who is given, through faith, to the fully consecrated believer. The resultant life of Christian holiness is known as perfect love or Christian perfection . . . though there are human conditions and responses necessary to its reception, sanctification is all grace, is not by works that a person does. (Carter, 1983, p. 521)

A human role in this stage of sanctification may be described more as a response to God's work than as human effort. Charles Carter (1983), a Wesleyan theologian writes, "the response required for entire sanctification is consecration and faith" (p. 564). However, there is also the process of "growth in grace," i.e., a more rapid progress of grace, after the event of entire sanctification that includes "the development of the skills of Christian living" (Carter, p. 563).

Fetters (1992), also a Wesleyan, emphasizing synergistic holy living, refers to human participation using the term "appropriation" when he writes, "The believer will appropriate the power of the Holy Spirit, thereby making progress in practical sanctification" (p. 506). By using the concepts of responding and appropriating, Wesleyans see sanctification as primarily God's work with believers involved at a significant but primarily passive level of involvement.

This fits the Wesleyan view of sanctification as a sequence of events. It begins at justification ("initial sanctification") and is perfected by a "second work of grace" ("second blessing"), resulting in "Christian perfection," "perfect love" or "entire sanctification." Sanctification begins at the moment of the new birth; entire sanctification is the experience of being made perfect in love" (Wood, 1988, p. 96). However, the resulting holy life involves the believer, by the power of the Holy Spirit, participating in "a lifelong process of growth in grace and ever increasing Christlikeness" (Fetters, 1992, p. 505).

Holiness View

The Holiness view holds to sanctificational synergism with emphasis on the Spirit's work and holy living. According to J. Rodman Williams (1990), a Pentecostal theologian, the quest for holiness is "not a movement *toward* sanctification (for believers are already holy) but a growth *in* it, a gradual process of transformation" (p. 89). Sanctification is primarily the work of the Triune God: The Father is the source, Jesus Christ is the agent, and the Holy Spirit is the energizer of sanctification. Yet, it is also the task of man.

> God does not work without our involvement. It is not that God does so much, say 50 percent, whereas man is called upon to accomplish the rest, the other 50 percent. It is, rather, *God all the way through man all the way.* (Williams, p. 102)

According to Russell Spittler (1988, pp. 135–137), professor and Pentecostal scholar, within the Holiness tradition lies the oldest form of Pentecostalism, a Wesleyan variety. This group holds to the idea of sanctification as a "second definite work" following conversion. But they also added the baptism of the Holy Spirit, accompanied with the speaking in tongues as a third distinct experience for Christians providing empowerment for service.

Another group, Baptistic or Reformed Pentecostals, merged the two alleged post-conversion experiences (sanctification and baptism in the Holy Sprit) into one experience called the baptism of the Holy Spirit. In this baptism, "sanctification . . . was viewed along Reformed lines, progressing from conversion to death (or Second Coming, whichever was to come first)" (Spittler, 1988, p. 136).

Spittler indicates that the Pentecostal view of human participation in sanctification is included in *obedience* though this obedience has often "led to a legalistic type of piety configured along the lines of rigoristic ethics: avoid theaters, dances, gambling, smoking, drinking" and other practices (pp. 142–143). Other statements of obedience and human involvement include dying to sin and living for righteousness.

Anglican View

The Anglican view expressed by W. H. Griffith Thomas (1930) sees sancti-fication as judicial, "sanctified in Christ," and practical, "a work being done in us now by the Holy Spirit…the life-long progressive Sanctification, or walking in purity and practical holiness" (p. 209). He is concerned about an emphasis on works in sanctification apart from faith. So human participation includes state-ments cautioning the Christian to not abandon the "one great principle of faith" that is to permeate all of life including practical sanctification.

This brief summary of the views on human participation in sanctification by various theological traditions indicates that each one supports a role for the be-liever in sanctification. The role varies depending on the tradition and perhaps within the tradition.

But, these differences do not diminish the general notion of synergism within each view. However, there may be those who find fault with this view of sanctification as being synergistic. I now defend my claim against these poten-tial defeaters.

A Defense of Sanctificational Synergism

For sake of clarity, I put forth the following denials.

1. Advocating sanctificational synergism does not mean that I am claiming that synergism involves a co-equal responsibility for both God and humans. Both agents have responsibilities that are different and essential for sanctificational growth (1 Cor 3:5–7; Gal 5:22–23; 1 Thess 5:23; Phil 1:6).
2. I am not claiming that humans have the same power as God does to produce sanctification. As will be examined in the next chapter, hu-man effort has an indirect role affecting belief, desires, and behavior while God has the power to directly affect humans.
3. I am not claiming that this model is appropriate for describing re-demption. It is limited to proposing an explanation of sanctification alone. Clearly, redemption is God's work alone, in which the sinner does not (and can not) contribute. Saving faith is the only response to God's work of redemption that results in salvation (Rom 3:24, 11:6; Gal 2:21; Eph 2:8).
4. I am not advocating the claim that the believer must put forth effort in order to remain justified. The issues of eternal security and the perseverance of the believer are for another discussion. This discus-sion of the relationship of human participation and God's work (syn-ergism) must be limited to sanctification.

There are other problematic issues raised by some theologians related to human participation in sanctification. The first issue is the notion that any human participation demonstrates works-righteousness and therefore is Pelagian. Hodge (1946) notes two key principles of Pelagianism (p. 250):

1. Pelagians believe that individuals live free from sin. "The nature of man is uninjured by the fall, so that men are free from sin until by voluntary transgression they incur guilt."
2. Pelagians believe that individuals have the innate ability to obey God. "Our natural powers, since, as well as before the fall, are fully competent to render complete obedience to the law."

One who upholds sanctificational synergism could respond by clarifying the distinction between justification and sanctification. Corresponding to the principles above, Demarest (1997) writes:

(1) [J]ustification is the legal declaration of right standing before God (imputed righteousness), whereas sanctification is the Spirit's work of making believers holy (imparted righteousness). (2) Justification is an instantaneous event, whereas sanctification is a lifelong process. And (3) justification allows for no degrees, whereas sanctification admits degrees. In terms of their inner unity, justification issues in sanctification, thereby eliminating the error of cheap grace. And sanctification is grounded in justification, thereby avoiding the heresy of works-righteousness. (p. 401)

The believer has been regenerated to render obedience to Christ possible. Thus, by God's grace and in faith, the believer's effort can be expended even though that effort does not earn merit with God. (Merit cannot be earned by the sinner and is unnecessary for the believer as it has been gained through Jesus Christ.)

Another argument against sanctificational synergism states that human participation tends toward legalism so should be rejected. Anglican theologian Thomas (1930) writes that

The supreme spiritual danger of the Christian life is legalism, for there is an inevitable tendency to assume that although justification is by faith, sanctification is somehow by struggle . . . making the believer feel the he cannot possibly be sanctified unless largely aided by his own efforts. (p. 209)

That an action is not performed properly does not argue for ceasing the action. Legalism is tied to activity. But that does not mean that all activity is legalistic. Sanctification cannot take place apart from human participation. However, only human activity accompanied by dependence on the Holy Spirit's power will be effective for spiritual growth. Sanctification is by faith and all efforts are engaged by faith as well, that is, faith in God's ability to empower one's activity for sanctificational growth.

A third potential problem might be stated as this: human participation tends to undermine God's sovereign ability and work by elevating man's ability and work. It is a man-centered system diminishing God's control.

In chapter three a presentation of the roles of God and human free will in sanctification will be given. I will leave a detailed response to this issue for that chapter. It is not the purpose of this study to explain the sovereignty of God as it relates to human effort. However, considering the discussion to this point, one must be challenged to acknowledge that, at some level, human effort in sanctification is necessary. This in no way diminishes God's sovereignty. The belief in some human participation does not mean that humans "take charge" of their own spiritual lives. A proper understanding of human participation will never lead one to conclude that believers are "in charge" of their own "self-sanctification" while ignoring God's control of the process.

There have been attempts at finding ways to explain divine and human roles in sanctification without limiting God's sovereign work. Frame (2002, pp. 154–159) seeks to explain the divine-human roles in the Christian's life (which will be applied to sanctification) by proposing the following models:

1. Pilot and copilot: both play roles but the model fails because only one pilot is directing the plane at any time.

2. Teacher and classroom: teacher is in control, providing guidelines and syllabus, but does not cause every action of every student; this model works for a libertarian view (Frame states that God does set boundaries like a teacher, but also has the power to control every thought, word, and deed of those under his lordship, so this model fails for him.)

3. Primary and secondary cause: A affects B which in turn causes effect on C; A is primary/remote cause of C while B is secondary/proximate cause of C; God often works through secondary causes. (Frame believes this model is weak because God's involvement with creation is in some sense always direct.)

4. Commander and troops: emphasizing God's authority and control through commands or speaking; (Frame fails to mention the role of the troops in this model.) Might be best model for sanctificational synergism—commander and troops must work together for victory with troops submitting to commander.

5. Author and characters in a story: Author is in full control of characters but seeks to make them and their events fit together in a coherent and artistic way; two causal chains operate at different levels—the author's and the characters' (similar to # 3). (Frame supports this model.)

Perhaps a sixth model would be appropriate—a jazz band. The leader of the band controls the musical selections and order; guides the tempo, interpretation, and quality of each selection; yet there is a freedom for the musician to improvise and engage mind, body, heart, and will in the "performance" while following the director's lead. The musicians are responsible to practice individually, rehearse together, live and perform in harmony, cooperate with the director, and create something wonderful together. They are not free to do whatever they want as the score, director, and the musical environment places parameters on them. However, they are free to play what is written and free to be innovative when appropriate. Their goal is to become such players that the music simply flows through them in response to and in harmony with the other players and the director.

This seems to be an appropriate analogy of sanctificational synergism with God as the band leader and believers as members of the band. This portrayal of synergism recognizes God's supervisory and directive role in the process while acknowledging the necessity for the musicians to play (i.e., participate). Without both kinds of participants there will be no effective spiritual expression or experience.

Conclusion

This chapter on sanctificational synergism concludes with statements by two theologians who recognize the essential role of believers in progressive sanctification. Moreover, both also seem to agree that this role includes the intentional engagement of heart and mind. The Reformed theologian Heppe (1978) writes, "Subjectively considered the nature of sanctification is man's effort, lasting his whole life, to live in thought, word, and action solely according to God's good pleasure and for His glory" (p. 570).

Thomas Oden (1994), a Methodist theologian, summarizes this chapter and leads into the next.

> Grace can only become habituated in moral character if it has first become actually offered and received. Actual grace, the divine gift enabling persons to perform acts beyond their natural powers, is distinguished from the grace of habituation by which sporadic actions are brought into recurrent patterns of willing.
>
> The Christian life is a continuing habituation in the reception of justifying grace. The will may move increasingly toward a sustained, habituated condition of receiving grace. What may have been a transient awareness at the first moment of receiving justifying grace gradually may become a more enduring, habituated condition, a more permanent state of free consent sustained by sanctifying grace through Word and Sacrament.
>
> Sanctifying grace is viewed by medieval Scholastics as working through habituation by forming behavior into stable patterns of responsiveness in the way of holiness so as to reflect the divine sonship. . . . This habituation is enabled by the Spirit through Word and Sacrament, and cannot be acquired simply or naturally by practice.
>
> Though Lutheran and Reformed Protestants may brace at such language, fearing that it might subtly turn God's grace into a human performance, it is upon careful inspection much closer to deeper Protestant intentionality than often imagined. (pp. 219–220)

I claim in this chapter that progressive sanctification is a work of God but not a work in which he engages apart from human involvement. Sanctificational synergism finds support in the biblical and theological literature despite some concerns.

CHAPTER 3

AN EXAMINATION OF THE BELIEVER'S CAPABILITY TO PARTICIPATE IN SANCTIFICATIONAL GROWTH

There is ongoing debate related to the doctrine of sanctification regarding the significance of and interaction between God's work and human participation in progressive sanctification. Chapter two supports the notion that it is essential that believers involve themselves in God's work (i.e., sanctificational synergism) of sanctificational growth since this process is not automatic. This was primarily a theological argument supported by Scripture. In this chapter, I examine the believer's ability to participate in sanctificational growth. The sources used are primarily philosophical while integrating these sources with theological works.

This chapter addresses the issue of the believer's capability to participate in sanctification. I argue that Christians are able to be involved in the sanctificational process because they possess free will. In other words, believers have the capability to make choices and to determine their actions demonstrating their life in Christ and obedience to Scripture. For example, in volitional freedom believers are able to yield themselves to the Spirit, exercise good choices, and establish good habits, all of which enable spiritual growth. Thus, the first part of this chapter is a discussion regarding the believer's ability to participate in sanctificational growth.

The second part of this chapter examines the claim that believers, possessing this capacity, are able to engage in the process of belief and character development resulting in sanctificational growth. The chapter presents a brief survey of the elements (viz., worldview, beliefs, and desires) that affect the believer's ability to grow spiritually.

Following the examination of these elements, I examine the indirect nature of belief formation as it affects character formation. Since character is commonly understood as one's system of beliefs and desires that, generally speaking, changes only gradually, I also examine how beliefs and desires are formed and changed.

The Believer's Free Will

"As traditionally conceived," writes philosophy professor Thomas Pink (1998), "the will is the faculty of choice or decision, by which we determine which actions we shall perform" (p. 720). As our discussion will bear out, believers (as with all humans) possess this faculty.

Regenerated Will

Due to misconceptions regarding the will after conversion, I suggest that though this faculty was tainted by sin due to the fall of humanity, the will, due to regeneration can function with the power of contrary choice. As theologians Lewis and Demarest (1996) write:

> People with Spirit-renewed wills need not yield to sin's enticements. Their No" can mean "No!" As the disciplined exercise good choices and acts, holy habits are formed. They grow in acting, not according to the flesh, but according to the Spirit. . . . Christians are freed from sin to determine actions in harmony with their new moral nature. (pp. 208–209)

Lewis and Demarest (1996, p. 96) propose to differentiate the freedom of the will according to four distinct eras. 1) Before the Fall, Adam and Eve experienced freedom not only as the power of responsible self-determination but also as a power of contrary choice. 2) Since the Fall, the unregenerate freely determine themselves in accord with their depraved natures. 3) At present, the regenerate, in addition to the old fleshly nature, have a new spiritual nature. The regenerate now have the power of contrary choice. 4) In the eternal state, the believer's freedom will be a fully sanctified nature like Christ's. Christians will only make choices that obey God and will no longer have the freedom of contrary choice.

If valid, these distinctions help clarify the believer's present capability or power of choice to please and obey God that the unregenerate do not posses. Demarest (1997, p. 298) notes the following results of Holy Spirit regeneration:

1. Intellectually, regeneration enables minds of sinners once blind and ignorant of spiritual truths to comprehend the things of God (1Cor 2:12, 14–16; 2 Cor 4:4, 6; Col 3:10). The new birth affects the renewal of the human capacity to know, love, and affirm God's purposes.
2. Volitionally, the new birth liberates believers' wills from moral bondage, enabling them to affirm and pursue kingdom values (Rom 6:13; Phil 2:13; 2 Thess 3:5).
3. Emotionally, regeneration initiates the reintegration of disordered affections and feelings (Rom 8:15).
4. Morally and ethically, regenerate believers are freed from depraved and enslaving passions. Christians can become more like Christ in thought, word, and deed (Gal 5:19–23)

5. Relationally, the new birth establishes genuine fellowship with the triune God (1Cor 1:9; Eph 2:22; 1 John 1:3) and meaningful relationships with other believers (Rom 12:5; Eph 2:14–15, 19–20).

As a result of regeneration, believers now have the freedom and ability to make choices that contribute to their growth in sanctification whereas before regeneration they were unable to do so.

Free Will

Free will describes the ability or power of a person to choose a course of action which he or she is then able to carry out.

> A man has free will if he is often in positions like these: he must now speak or now be silent, and he *can* now speak and *can* now remain silent; he must attempt to rescue a drowning child or else go for help, and he is *able* to attempt to rescue the child and *able* to go for help; he must now resign his chairmanship or else lie to the members, and he has it within his power to resign and he has it within his power to lie. 'Free will', then is to be defined in terms of 'can'. . . the concept of the power or ability of an agent to act. (van Inwagen, 1993, p. 8)

The significance of free will, from a Christian perspective, is stated by professor of theology William Ury (1996) as 1) resulting from the image of God in humans, 2) requiring responsibility in making moral choices, 3) distinguishing humans from animals, and 4) not diminishing the sovereignty of God. He writes:

> The created image of God carries with it awesome responsibility and glory. It includes the ability to make meaningful moral choices. . . . By grace, the freedom to use a created will as a moral agent is one of the key biblical distinctions between humans and the rest of the created order. The sovereignty of God is deepened in a radically personal way when creation is climaxed by persons who possess wills that can choose to either obey or disobey, to love or not to love. True sovereignty is neither arbitrary nor coercive; it allows other wills. (p. 818)

In discussing free will in a Christian context, confusion may arise over the relationship of the divine will and human responsibility. The uncertainty stems from, in part, the belief one has about the freedom of the will. Is it really up to us to decide which actions we perform, is God the only agent whose will is accomplished, or is it a combination of both? Before these questions are addressed, we must understand the three distinct views concerning free will.

Each of the three following views seeks to address the problem of free will.

1. Libertarianism views one's self as the originator of one's actions.

> It is the theory that claims that some actions are exempt from the causal laws, in which the individual is the sole (or decisive) cause of the act, the act originating *ex nihilo* (out of nothing), cut off from all other causes but the self's origination. (Pojman, 1991, p. 381)

Libertarianism is the view that real freedom requires a type of control over one's action or one's will. The person or agent is the absolute originator of his own actions (Moreland and Craig, 2003, p. 270) in most cases.

2. Determinism (Hard) explains away free choice by holding that all choices, including future choices, have already been set in advance. It is described as "the view that for every event that happens, there are conditions such that, given them, nothing else could have happened" (Moreland and Craig, 2003, p. 268) and "the theory that everything in the universe (or at least the macroscopic universe) is entirely determined by causal laws, so that whatever happens at any given moment is the effect of some antecedent cause" (Pojman, 1991, p. 381). According to this view, people are determined to choose and do everything that they ever choose and do.

3. Compatibilism (Soft Determinism) is the theory that tries to combine the best of libertarianism and determinism. "It says, though admitting everything is determined, that we can still be said to be free insofar as we can still act voluntarily" (Pojman, p. 381). It is a belief that both freedom and determinism are true and thus, compatible.

The purpose for this discussion is to understand the views that are compatible with human participation in sanctification. It seems that libertarianism and compatibilism can support human participation. Within both these views, the person is able to make choices which are free (in the sense specified by the respective theory) and has the power to take action that leads to sanctificational growth. This may be what is seen in Romans 6:12–14 as believers are given the choice of presenting themselves to sin as instruments of unrighteousness or of presenting themselves to God as instruments of righteousness. Neither sin nor God determine the choice though the resources of being in union with Christ have been made available. Believers are commanded to make the choice themselves. They can obey God's command and defeat sin's dominion or disobey God and continue to allow sin to influence them. The concern here is not so much to untangle the theological and philosophical details of libertarianism and determinism but to suggest that either theory comports well with the claim that believers can play a role in their sanctification. But what about determinism?

As already noted, determinism explains away free choice by holding to the notion that all mental and physical actions are caused by conditions outside a person's control. An individual, then, becomes a conduit or channel for a series of causes in place from before one's birth and continuing into the future, even after death. In this scenario, freedom of the will does not exist and humans may be seen as merely puppets or robots. When applied to sanctification, determinists would hold that believers are passive recipients of sanctificational causes and do not participate in the process. We have seen from Scripture and theology that this notion of passivity would be difficult to defend.

Philosophy professor and author Dallas Willard (1998), provides an illustration of free will which he calls a "kingdom." Every individual oversees a "kingdom," "queendom," or "government"—"a realm that is uniquely our own, where our choice determines what happens. Here is a truth that reaches into the deepest part of what it is to be a person." Instead of believing that this kingdom emboldens human pride (i.e., our attempt to rule ourselves and others), Willard states that humans were created with this "likeness of God" and it is, in part, what makes us human. Without this will, we would cease to be a person. Persons with no will "would be reduced to completely passive observers who count for nothing, who make no difference" (p. 22).

He describes an individual's "kingdom" as

> the extent of one's effective will. Whatever we genuinely have the say over is *in* our kingdom. And our having the say over something is precisely what places it within our kingdom. In creating human beings God made them rule, to reign, to have dominion in a limited sphere. (p. 21)

However, this governance is to take place in union with God and his kingdom.

> God equipped us for this task by framing our nature to function in a conscious, personal relationship of interactive responsibility *with* him. We are meant to exercise our "rule" only in union with God, as he acts with us. He intended to be our constant companion or co-worker in the creative enterprise of life on earth . . . We discover the effectiveness of his rule *with* us precisely in the details of day–to–day existence. (p. 22–24)

The details and significance of this union with God in Christ will be examined in chapter five. But as has already been discussed in chapter two, believers only progress in sanctificational growth and life in the kingdom as they work with God in a spiritual partnership. Working with God entails the ability to make choices aligned with his will, to establish habits according to his word, and to take actions obedient to his calling. Having introduced philosophers' explanations of free will, I now turn to some theologians whose writings also support the believer's ability to make free choices and in this way participate in sanctificational growth.

Free Will Supported by Select Evangelical Theologians

There seems to be agreement among many contemporary evangelical theologians regarding the existence of free will in the believer. These theologians do not agree on how human free will interacts with God's will though they support its crucial place in enabling participation in sanctificational growth. Theologian Millard J. Erickson (1985) asserts that either libertarianism or compatibilism is consistent with viewing humans as created with free will.

> [M]an would not be man if he did not have free will. . . . whether humans are free in the sense assumed by Arminians . . . or free in a sense not inconsistent with God's having rendered certain what is to happen (compatibilistic free-

dom), God's having made man as he purposed means that man has certain capacities (e.g., the capacities to desire and act). (p. 424)

Theologian and philosophy professor Gordon Lewis and theologian Bruce
Demarest (1996) claim that believers, in the power of the Spirit, are able to
"make *Christlike moral decisions* and keep them" (p. 208). They write as libertarians.

> The freedom to decide on what we know and love as right is one aspect of the
> inner person; the ability to do this is another. Believers need not remain en-
> slaved to sinful ways. . . . Believing men and women are not mere victims of
> their families, schools, churches, or communities. They are responsible agents
> to determine their own activities in accord with the desires exemplified in the
> moral teaching of Scripture. (pp. 208–209)

Another theologian, Wayne Grudem (1994) a compatibilist, states that human existence entails the essentiality of divine control along with freedom.

> Scripture nowhere says that we are "free" in the sense of being outside of
> God's control or of being able to make decisions that are not caused by any-
> thing . . . Nor does it say we are "free" in the sense of being able to do right on
> our own apart from God's power. But we are free in the greatest sense that any
> creature of God could be free—we make *willing* choices, choices that have *real*
> *effects*. We are aware of no restraints on our will from God when we make de-
> cisions. We must insist that we have the power of *willing* choice; otherwise we
> will fall into the error of fatalism or determinism and thus conclude that our
> choices do not matter, or that we cannot really make willing choices. On the
> other hand, the kind of freedom that is demanded by those who deny God's
> providential control of all things, a freedom to be outside of God's sustaining
> and controlling activity, would be impossible if Jesus Christ is indeed "continu-
> ally carrying along things by his word of power." . . . If this is true, then to be
> outside of that providential control would simply be not to exist! An absolute
> "freedom," totally free of God's control, is simply not possible in a world
> providentially sustained and directed by God himself. (p. 331)

These theologians agree that believers have the power to choose. They differ on whether this power originates from believers themselves or in conjunction
with God's determination. Nevertheless, in either case, free will is seen as an
essential component of human existence and by implication an essential element
of human participation in sanctificational growth.

Character and Free Will

However, more than free will is necessary in making these kinds of choices
that lead to sanctificational growth. Philosophy professor Galen Strawson (1998)
introduces this notion.

> 'Free will' is the conventional name of a topic that is best discussed without
> reference to the will. Its central questions are 'What is it to act (or choose)

freely?' and 'What is it to be morally responsible for one's actions (or choices)?' These two questions are closely connected, for freedom of action [or choice] is necessary for moral responsibility, even if it is not sufficient. (p. 743)

The last sentence is significant as Strawson notes the necessity of freedom in moral choices and actions but also notes that, as far as moral responsibility goes, more than freedom is needed. Philosophy professor David Ciocchi (1993) agrees:

> Free will is a necessary, but not a *sufficient*, condition for moral responsibility. . . . Free will is not a sufficient condition for responsibility because it is possible for a person to freely choose to do something yet not be morally responsible for the outcome of that act [viz., innocently drinking punch that has been poisoned]. . . . Second, a believer in free will need not suppose that *all* human behavior is freely chosen [viz., reflex actions, actions done under the influence of drugs, mental illness] . . . Third . . . even though some human behavior is not freely chosen . . . a believer in free will affirms that *much* or *most* of the behavior of human beings is either freely chosen or the result of earlier free choices . . . the upshot of this is that the believer in free will regards freedom and moral responsibility as the typical or *paradigmatic* human condition. This fits the biblical teaching that God is the judge of us all: *all* human beings, not just most of us, will be held accountable for the lives we have lived. (p. 89)

These philosophers claim that free will is necessary but insufficient for moral responsibility. What additional component is necessary? I believe one's character plays a role in responsible behavior. Character can be defined as "roughly a more-or-less structured set of beliefs and desires" (Ciocchi, 1993, p. 93). Both libertarians and compatibilists agree that a person's character is related to decisions that are made. The two views differ, however, in the role that character plays in these choices. Compatibilists believe that one's character will determine choices that are made since they believe that individuals are their character. Libertarians, however, believe that character has a say, though not the final say, in choices that are made and also that character determines the range of options from which free choices will be made (Ciocchi, 1993, p. 93). Our concern here is to show that the two views supporting human participation agree that one's character has a role but not to probe deeper into these role differences.

Therefore, in both views that support human participation in sanctificational growth, character influences the decisions and actions of the person. In other words believers' choices are always made within the context of their whole character. The onus for the believer, then, is to develop a character that so informs and influences decision-making that growth in Christlikeness becomes the certain course of one's life.

Key Factors Affecting Character Development and Sanctificational Growth

Since decisions are made within the context of one's character, the believer's free will does not independently operate in contributing to sanctificational growth. As individuals make choices, there is an interaction with other faculties of the human being in order that sanctification may take place. Willard (2002) states:

> Our actions *always* arise out of the *interplay* of the universal factors in human life: spirit, mind, body, social context, and soul. Action never comes from the movement of the will alone. Often—perhaps usually—what we do is not an outcome of deliberate choice and mere act of the will, but is more of a *relenting* to pressure on the will from one or more of the dimensions of the self. The understanding of this is necessary for the understanding and practice of spiritual formation, which is bound to fail if it focuses on the will alone. (p. 39)

Ciocchi (1993) sees this interplay as an indication of compatibilism which presupposes that the agent himself is the locus of free will, and is virtually if not precisely identical to his character. He writes:

> Given the agent's character and the particular circumstances in which he finds himself, he cannot fail to have a preference, a particular option that matters more to him at this time than any other option. His personal reason or reasons for choosing to act on this option will prevail over any reasons he may have for other options, if any. To put it another way, whatever matters most to the agent will *determine* which choice he makes. This will be his choice, under his control, "up to him," for his character determines his choice, and he *is* his character. (p. 93)

Even in libertarianism, an individual may choose freely yet "his desires or beliefs may influence his choice or play an important role in his deliberations" (Moreland and Craig, 2003, p. 270).

If character plays such an essential role in free choices, it is important to understand its nature and, for our purposes, its relationship to sanctificational growth. Philosopher Richard Swinburne (1998) defines character as one's "system of desires and beliefs" (p. 91) and explains the nature of character.

> [W]hich action an agent will do is limited and influenced by his system of beliefs and desires, his continuing mental states. He will do the action which, he believes, will, most probably, attain his goals; and he can only choose to do that action (if there is one) which he believes to be overall the best of those open to him. But other things are not necessarily equal; an agent is also subject to *desire*; some actions come more naturally to him than do others. Whether to yield to desire or to pursue the best lies within the agent's free choice. An agent's system of beliefs and desires is a continuing one. Gradually beliefs change or are forgotten, but most beliefs continue for quite a while. Some de-sires are of short duration and for short-term goals (e.g., for a drink now), but there are

many desires which are long term and long lasting. Agents thus have a continuing system of beliefs and desires subject only to gradual change. (p. 262)

The remainder of this chapter will be an examination of worldview, belief,
and desire—their nature and formation—as key components to character development. However, as a reminder of the bigger picture regarding sanctification, I
need to state that a developed character, though necessary to sanctification, is
not sufficient for sanctification. God's part in the sanctificational work must
always be recognized even though our primary discussion here relates to the
believer's role in character development.

Worldview

The first component of character development to be examined is one's
worldview. This concept has been chosen since it entails significant elements
that contribute to character development such as one's beliefs, practices, and
view of reality.

Generally speaking, the term "worldview" refers to a person's basic view of
life or interpretation of reality (Naugle, 2002, p. 260). James Sire (2004), author
and lecturer on worldviews, provides a comprehensive definition of worldview.

A worldview is a commitment, a fundamental orientation of the heart, that can
be expressed as a story or in a set of presuppositions (assumptions which may
be true, partially true or entirely false) which we hold (consciously or subcon-
sciously, consistently or inconsistently) about the basic constitution of reality,
and that provides the foundation on which we live and move and have our being. (p. 122)

Sire's use of the term "commitment" seems to imply an emotional and intellectual fidelity to an idea or the dedication to a course of action both of which
denote a long–term commitment. This "orientation of the heart" also implies that
the choices one makes will generally align with one's worldview. Even though,
by possessing the capacity of free will one has the power to make choices, they
are made out of basic commitments or orientations of one's heart. This basic
heart orientation entails a set of assumptions the truth of which cannot be as-
sumed, Sire continues to explain. These assumptions seem to relate to the idea
of belief implied by his use of the word "hold." Thus, in his definition, there is a
relationship between one's beliefs and one's view of reality. He also notes that
though these beliefs are maintained, they are not always ones of which we are
aware or which we practice consistently. It seems that in becoming aware of
unconscious beliefs or in examining the coherence of belief and reality, our
worldview is given an opportunity to better reflect reality and to provide a better
framework from which to live.

Sire's definition also emphasizes that one's worldview entails one's beliefs
about reality and beliefs about how one should live. If one believes in the reality
of the supernatural, that belief provides the basis for certain actions. If that belief

is part of one's worldview, one will interpret reality in the light of the belief in the supernatural.

That the assumptions in one's worldview may be hidden or inconsistent suggests that people's view of reality is often inaccurate and therefore in need of constant change. The formation of beliefs to better reflect reality will be examined later in this chapter.

This understanding of worldview also suggests that every person is unique in their worldview. Professor of philosophy Michael Palmer (1998) adds the notion of personal uniqueness to his description of worldview.

> Our core beliefs and practices form a point of view or perspective that is distinctively ours. This distinctive perspective constitutes our *worldview*; our various core beliefs and practices are the *elements* of that worldview. A worldview, then, is a set of beliefs and practices that shape a person's approach to the most important issues in life. Through our worldview, we determine priorities, explain our relationship to God and fellow human beings, assess the meaning of events, and justify our actions. (p. 24)

Professor of cultural anthropology Charles Kraft (1989) agrees when he describes an individual's worldview as "comprised of his or her own set of assumptions, beliefs, values, and commitments that differ from those of other individuals" (p. 81). (Though Palmer describes a worldview as a set of beliefs and practices, the emphasis in this discussion will center on beliefs.)

If these descriptions of a worldview are valid, how can our beliefs be formed so they better reflect reality in our thoughts and practices? How are our beliefs, values, or commitments formed so that they shape our perspective on the most important issues of life? It seems that believers who are maturing will be constantly adjusting their worldview to better embrace reality.

First, we must understand the difficulty of this "reorientation." Kraft (2001) explains that a worldview can be altered, but only as one is willing to question current assumptions.

> In terms of their worldview *a people organizes their life and experiences into an explanatory whole that they seldom (if ever) question unless some of its assumptions are challenged* by experiences that the people cannot interpret from within that framework. (p. 102)

Here, Kraft addresses the problem of people changing their worldview due to their biases in perceptions of reality ("blind spots") that influence and control their worldview. One's worldview interprets experiences until those experiences cannot be explained by that worldview framework. A dissonance is created. In this environment of conflicting or confusing orientation with reality, often brought about by different experiences, one's worldview may be questioned and altered.

A reason to change one's worldview is that it carries biases unique to the individual. But to lessen one's biases, some core beliefs need to be challenged by beliefs outside one's "plausibility structure," that is, "the set of ideas the person either is or is not willing to entertain as possibly true" (Moreland, 1997, pp.

75–76). One's plausibility structure is formed out of beliefs one already has or beliefs one refuses to accept. It is an existing condition that is used to allow or disallow the possibility that an idea may be true. Yet, for a worldview to better reflect reality, there is a need for individuals to consider the possibility that a belief might be true. Moreland (1997) writes:

> I will never be able to change my life if I cannot even entertain the belief needed to bring about that change. By "entertain a belief" I mean to consider the *possibility* that the belief *might* be true. If you are hateful and mean to someone at work you will have to change what you believe about the person before you will treat him or her differently. But if you cannot even entertain the thought that he or she is a good person worthy of kindness, you won't change. (p. 75)

Another reason to change one's worldview is because one's view of reality is always incomplete and selective, according to Kraft (1979, p. 26). This is true, he claims, since "we see reality not as it is but always from inside our heads" (p. 29). If limitations to understanding reality are always present there must be some way to reduce these limitations so that a more comprehensive view of reality can be developed. Later in this chapter I will examine the process of belief formation that addresses this issue. Here, I simply suggest that these limitations can be gradually altered or eliminated by entertaining beliefs that might be true. Therefore, believers must always be in the process of formulating new beliefs to better match reality. And if they do not participate in this process they maintain a limited understanding of reality.

When applied to an individual's beliefs regarding free will, individuals may bring an insufficient understanding to the free will decision-making process—not only in their beliefs concerning free will but also in their understanding of how free will operates in the change process. One's belief in the role of free will in decision making and sanctificational growth will contribute to his or her view of reality related to intentionality and passivity. Here we see the interplay of worldview and free will.

The basis for interpreting reality and viewing life is found in our beliefs. If I have a friend whose young boy dies of an incurable disease, I will try to understand his death (i.e., interpret that reality) according to certain beliefs such as the nature of God (Does he exist? Where was he? Why didn't he prevent this suffering?), creation (How did we get here? For what purpose did this boy live?), human beings (What is human nature? Did this boy have a soul?), and death (What happens after human beings die?). One's view of reality is constituted by a set of beliefs that inform one's experiences of life. A closer examination of beliefs is warranted.

Beliefs

Beliefs, as has been stated, are a key component to character development and therefore, to sanctification. "Beliefs are views about how the world is" (Swinburne, 1998, p. 55). Thus, beliefs inform our understanding of the world around us including the spiritual world. Swinburne (1997) claims that "beliefs are [our] map of the world, what [we] hold to be true about it" (p. 122).

Moreland & Rae (2000) describe belief as

> a person's view, accepted to varying degrees of strength, of how things really are. If a person has a belief (e.g., that it is raining), then that belief serves as the basis for the person's tendency or readiness to act as if the thing believed were really so (e.g., one gets an umbrella). Thus beliefs are not dispositions to behave but are the grounds for such dispositions. (p. 159)

What is entailed in belief? Of what do beliefs consist? Moreland (1997) claims that there are three aspects of belief:

1. The *content* of belief is what is believed (e.g., about God, politics, priorities, or education). Moreland connects belief with truth and responsibility.

   > As far as reality is concerned, what matters is not whether I like a belief or how sincere I am in believing it but whether or not the belief is true. I am responsible for what I believe and, I might add, for what I refuse to believe because the content of what I do or do not believe makes a tremendous difference to what I become and how I act. (p. 74)

2. The *strength* of belief is the degree to which one is convinced a belief is true; "it is not belief as such, but relative strength of belief that affects action" (Swinburne, 2001, p. 37). Moreland explains this notion further:

   > If you believe something, that does not mean you are certain that it is true. Rather, it means that you are at least more than 50 percent convinced the belief is true. If it were fifty-fifty for you, you wouldn't really have the belief in question. Instead, you would still be in a process of deciding whether or not you should adopt the belief. (p. 74)

3. The *centrality* of belief is "the degree of importance the belief plays in one's entire set of beliefs, that is, in your worldview" (Moreland, 1997, p. 74). The more central the belief the greater the impact on one's set of beliefs if that belief were abandoned. Moreland illustrates this concept.

   > My belief that prunes are good for me is fairly strong (even though I don't like the belief!), but it isn't very central for me. I could give it up and not have to abandon or adjust very many other beliefs I hold. But my beliefs in absolute morality, life after death, or the Christian faith are very central for me—more central now, in fact, than just after my conversion in 1968. If I were to lose these beliefs, my entire set of beliefs would undergo a radical reshuffling. (pp. 74–75)

Yet there are beliefs of which we are aware and others of which we are not as was discussed in the worldview section. Swinburne (2001) describes these two kinds of beliefs.

1. Standing beliefs: continuing mental state— "ones that we can have without currently being in any way aware of them; but they are mental in that we can, if we choose, become aware of them by a means not open to others" (p. 38).

2. Occurent beliefs: conscious mental state—"such that, if we are in those states, necessarily to some extent we are occurently aware of being in those states" (p. 38).

Perhaps Paul's use of "know" and "reckon" in the Romans 6:5–11 passage illustrates these meanings of belief. "Know" (v. 6) is in the present tense indicating contemporaneous action (Rogers and Rogers, 1998, p. 327) in which believers "keep on grasping and understanding" the following theological truth that expresses itself in the experiences of life (Schmitz, 1976, p. 401). The knowledge that "our old self was crucified with him in order that the body of sin might be brought to nothing, so that we would no longer be enslaved to sin" implies a standing belief that believers may or may not be aware of at any given moment but, as part of their worldview, shapes their view of reality (viz. that sin has no more dominion over them). However, Paul commands believers to bring this standing belief to mind with settled determination ("reckon," v. 11) and therefore live with their "dead-to-sin-and-alive-to-God" reality as a conscious mental belief in order to effectively deal with sin's power.

These two kinds of belief may also be seen in such passages as John 17:3 ("And this is eternal life, that they know you the only true God, and Jesus Christ whom you have sent"), Philippians 3:8–11 ("and be found in him . . . having a righteousness . . . which comes through faith in Christ . . . that I may know him"), and 1 John 5:13 ("I write these things to you who believe in the name of the Son of God that you may know that you have eternal life"). These passages imply that a relationship with God (i.e., "eternal life") involves both a conscious belief in Christ and his work and an ongoing belief in Christ and his work.

If beliefs are views about how the world really is then their place in shaping one's view of reality entailed in one's worldview can be seen. In fact, one's worldview and one's beliefs are similarly described as our map of what is considered true or real by Swinburne (1997) and Kraft (2001). Both beliefs and worldview relate to reality. And both can be changed to better understand and live reality.

What is the believer's view of how things really are? Do they believe the reality of their sins being forgiven and their possession of eternal life? Do they believe they are united to Christ and indwelt by the Holy Spirit? Do they see themselves as holy ones and followers of Jesus Christ? These beliefs, among many others, are the basis for living the Christian life and developing a Christlike character. The strength and centrality of these beliefs become an issue when related to their influence on one's worldview especially as these beliefs relate to sanctificational growth. Beliefs prove to be a key component to character development and therefore to sanctification. As Swinburne (1997) writes,

"An agent's beliefs . . . affect the way in which he executes his purposes . . . it follows that the agent will do the action which, it follows from his beliefs, will most probably attain his goal" (p. 128). If the goal is sanctificational growth, then beliefs regarding human and divine participation, union with Christ, the role of the Holy Spirit, free will, and sanctification will affect the actions believers take towards sanctificational growth.

But how are beliefs formed? Do I choose to believe what I want to believe as an act of the will? What is involved in the process of changing beliefs? I now address these questions.

Belief Formation

Believers are responsible, by indirect means, to develop beliefs that are true and to change false beliefs in order to grow in sanctification. Scripture seems to support this statement. By sowing bountifully (i.e., indirect means), giving as one has made up his or her mind, the believer learns (i.e., develop belief) that God is able to make his grace to abound sufficiently and enrich the believer in every way (2 Cor 9:6–15). "The righteous shall live by faith" and not by the law (i.e., means) for it is by faith in Christ that sinners are redeemed and it is by faith that the Spirit is received (i.e., belief) (Gal 3:10–14). It is by walking in the Spirit and not in the flesh (i.e., means) that Christlikeness is demonstrated (i.e., belief) (Gal 5:16–25). Believers are to "no longer walk as Gentiles do" but "be renewed in the spirit of your minds and [also] put on the new self, created after the likeness of God in true righteousness and holiness" (Eph 4:17–31).

Philosophers also support the claim that beliefs are formed indirectly. According to philosophy professor Louis Pojman (1986), there are five different positions on the direct relation of the will to belief acquisition, but states that "virtually everyone admits the will's indirect influence on belief formation" (p. viii). He continues to explain the relationship of belief and the will.

> Indirectly believing does involve the will . . . we cannot normally believe anything at all simply by willing to do so, for believing aims at truth and is not a basic act or a direct product of the will. If we could believe whatever we chose to believe simply by willing to do so, belief would not be about reality but about our wants. Nevertheless, the will does play an important indirect role in believing . . . Although believing is not an act, our acts determine the sorts of beliefs we end up with. (p. 180)

Swinburne (1997) agrees:
1. Belief is a passive and involuntary state. Belief is "a state in which you are, it is not a matter of doing something . . . [it is] a state in which you find yourself" (p. 126).
2. We cannot directly change our beliefs. Belief is a state "which you cannot change at will" (p. 126)
3. We can indirectly change our beliefs. "It is true that while I cannot change my beliefs at an instant, I can set about trying to change them over a period and I may have some success in this" (p. 127).

Swinburne (1997) also states that beliefs can be changed indirectly by a) looking for more evidence, b) seeking to cultivate a belief, or c) adopting new standards of assessing old evidence. He summarizes his position by stating that beliefs

> normally change (in a way unplanned by the subject) as a result of all his perceptions of the world, his thoughts about them, and the arguments which others give to him. A man's beliefs change in the light of the evidence to which he is exposed and his standards for assessing that evidence (which may or may not be rational ones). (p. 128)

But if beliefs are formed indirectly, that is, if one cannot simply will to believe something, how can individuals be held responsible for their beliefs? Pojman (1986) explains:

> It is primarily because we judge that our beliefs are to some significant degree the indirect results of our actions that we speak of being responsible for them. Although we cannot be said to be directly responsible for them, as though they were actions, we can be said to be indirectly responsible for many of them. If we had chosen differently, if we had been better moral agents, paid attention to the evidence, and so forth, we would have different beliefs than we in fact do have. (p. 180)

People are held responsible for their decisions because they, by their will, choose to consider reasons for and against certain actions. Moreland and Craig (2003) explain that this process of deliberation is called indirect doxastic voluntarism. It is "the idea that one's beliefs result from processes of deliberation in which one exercises freedom at various points along the way, in what one will or will not consider, how one will look at the issue, etc." (p. 277). In this way, people can influence their beliefs and are thus held responsible for their beliefs despite the indirect nature of belief formation.

In relating this discussion to sanctification, decision making is crucial to spiritual growth. Believers are free to make choices contrary to God's design for them. They are given the freedom of contrary choice. But they are also free to make choices that fulfill God's design. They are given instruction and power to make choices that please God and fulfill his will. Believers are responsible to consider evidence that is true (e.g., biblical wisdom and propositions), honorable, just, pure lovely, commendable, excellent, and praiseworthy (Phil 4:8). This process should be void of anxiety and marked by thankful prayer (Phil 4:4–7)

Thus, deliberation is an ongoing activity involving free will in the process resulting in the formation of beliefs. Decisions involving free will and character are necessary if goals are to be reached including the goal of sanctificational growth. According to Swinburne (1997), decisions are the means by which many people continue to pursue long-term goals; the decision is a reason to continue (p. 121). For example, choices to meditate on God's word, spend time with God in solitude, give sacrificially, practice God's presence, pray throughout the day, or forgive an enemy have the potential to sustain the believer's character development and to establish beliefs that provide a better and more comprehensive view of reality. The gradual change in one's beliefs leads to a gradual change in one's character.

Desires

Character is not formed by belief alone. As traditionally understood, character is the structured set of beliefs and desires. Having examined beliefs, we now look at desires. Desire is defined as "a certain felt inclination to do, have, avoid or experience certain things" (Moreland and Rae, 2000, p. 159). Swinburne (1997) describes desires and how we manage them.

> A 'desire' or 'want' . . . is a natural inclination to do some action with which an agent finds himself. We cannot (immediately) help our natural inclinations but what we can do is choose whether to yield to them, or resist them and do what we are not naturally inclined to do. When we resist our natural inclinations, we do so because we have reasons for action quite other than ones naturally described as the satisfaction of desire—e.g. we do the action because we believe that we ought to, or we believe it to be in our long-term interest. (p. 103)

He continues:

> What is a natural 'inclination'? It is a readiness (of which the agent can become aware in consciousness) spontaneously to do the action when, in the agent's belief, the opportunity arises—but for any belief he may have about the peripheral consequences and properties of the action, and but for any desire to do a rival action which the agent believes cannot be done at the same time. (p. 105)

The relationship of beliefs and desires are explained in these descriptions of desire. Swinburne believes that desires can be controlled by one's beliefs and by reasons other than those presented by the desire itself. For example, when given too much change by the grocery store clerk one must decide whether to act on the desire for pleasure (i.e., "getting what I deserve," or "beating the system") and keep the money or return it for reasons of honesty and integrity (i.e., principles of right and wrong) or accountability (i.e., someone is watching me). One's character (i.e., a set of beliefs and desires) will inform the decision that is made.

But if desires are simply natural inclinations to do an action when given the opportunity, how can one then be held responsible for acting on what is "natural?" As with beliefs, the responsibility is on individuals to make choices to do what will change their desires to better reflect reality or truth. Desires are to some degree an indirect result of our actions. Desires, therefore, can be changed as an indirect result of actions. The choices we make or the evidence that we accept (or reject) indirectly determine what desires we have.

Scripture seems to support this notion. By presenting oneself to God as one brought from death to life and as an instrument for righteousness (and conversely, not presenting oneself to sin as an instrument for unrighteousness), believers are able to "disobey" the passions/desires of sin (Rom 6:12–13). By walking in the Spirit, believers are able to control their desires as ones who have crucified the flesh and are able to manifest Christlike desires and characteristics (Gal 5:16–25). As obedient children (i.e., "preparing your minds for action and being sober–minded" while setting their hope on the coming of Christ), believers do not have to give in to the passions which characterized their "preconversion" lives, but can conduct themselves as holy ones with holy desires (1 Pet 1:13–16). These actions (i.e., "presenting," "walking," "obeying") indirectly affect desires and change them into desires that reflect God's reality. Good actions indirectly result in good desires.

Over time, therefore, as desires (and beliefs) are changed, one's character is changed also. Swinburne (1998) explains:

> A person's character is her system of desires and beliefs (principally moral beliefs); and just as it is good that agents have the choice of seeking to improve their beliefs or of not bothering to do so, so it is good that they should have the power to modify their desires over time. It is good that they be able to develop good desires and strengthen the best desires, (including, for example, the desire for knowledge); or allow themselves to be captured by bad desires. But . . . such character modification will involve a restriction of the kind and degree of free choice. In so far as we eliminate bad desires, our freedom of choice will be restricted to good alternatives.
>
> One way in which this could happen is the way it does happen in humans. Humans are so made that, by forcing themselves to do good actions when it is difficult, it becomes easier and easier to do them, until finally we desire to do them—our inclinations naturally lead us to do them. As Aristotle famously remarked, 'we become just by doing just acts, temperate by doing temperate acts, brave by doing brave acts'. We can so dedicate ourselves to doing good by constant commitment over time that bad desires cease to have influence over us. (pp. 92–93)

In other words, changed desires result from training oneself to act in corrective ways relative to those desires. "In general, one cannot change deeply embedded desires and behavioral patterns without some form of bodily or behavioral training . . . wrong behaviors (linked to wrong desires), can be corrected through practice" (Issler, 2000, p. 4). This training goes beyond "behavior modification" techniques that are primarily focused on behavior for the sake of changing behavior. Here, behavior is addressed for the sake of changing desires. The training of one's actions takes place over time and over time one's desires (and beliefs) can be changed. So, the whole character is indirectly affected by one's actions not just one's behavior.

Experientially, the practice of spiritual disciplines can be a means of changing wrong desires and growing in sanctification. Through practices that involve bodily actions such as fasting, solitude, study, or service, the body is trained and desires are changed while growth in sanctification takes place. Willard (1988) notes the responsibility of believers to indirectly affect their spirit or soul through spiritual disciplines.

What then are the specific roles of the spiritual disciplines? Their role rests upon the nature of the embodied human self – they are to *mold* and *shape* it. And our part in our redemption is, through specific and appropriate activities . . . We are to take this task with utmost seriousness and in the most literal of senses, since *no one*, not even God himself, *will do it for us*. That is the meaning of our freedom and of our responsibility. (pp. 92–93)

A more detailed discussion of the place of spiritual disciplines will be presented in chapter six. Mention of them here is to suggest a practical means whereby one's beliefs and desires can be changed as an indirect result of one's actions.

Conclusion

Believers have the capability to make choices which, when integrated with other components of the heart and mind, contribute to sanctificational growth. Thus, in this chapter I have argued that Christians are able to be involved in the sanctificational process because they possess free will. This claim is supported by libertarians and compatibilists as well as evangelical theologians. Believers have power, under the Lordship of Jesus Christ, to make choices and to determine their actions demonstrating their life in Christ and obedience to Scripture. For example, believers can decide to yield themselves to the Spirit (discussed in chapter five), learn to make good choices, and establish good habits which enable spiritual growth.

The second part of this chapter examined the claim that believers, possessing the capability to make decisions, can develop their character. It is agreed that character influences one's decisions whether one approaches free will as a libertarian or compatibilist. Character is traditionally understood as the set of one's beliefs and desires that are subject only to gradual change. One's "worldview" (i.e., view of reality), constituted by a set of beliefs, provides a framework for seeing the world and is inherently in need of change. By choosing actions that indirectly result in the formation of beliefs and desires, one's character is formed. One's character, in turn, influences one's choices. The interplay of these elements for character development and sanctificational growth is clearly evident. Believers are thus capable of implementing effective actions that will work to alter their character towards conformity to Christ's own character.

CHAPTER 4

AN EXAMINATION OF MARTIN FORD'S
CONCEPT OF PERSONAL AGENCY BELIEFS

We have examined the place of human participation in God's work of sanctification. Sanctificational growth is a synergistic work involving the intentional actions of believers along with the resources provided by God. Believers have some responsibility in their own spiritual growth primarily through forming beliefs and making choices from a transformed character. Having established that we are capable of forming beliefs, in this chapter I introduce a specific set of beliefs that will help believers function effectively in sanctificational growth. In this chapter I examine the concept of personal agency beliefs and suggest that these kinds of beliefs are essential to spiritual growth.

Martin Ford (1992), a writer in the field of educational psychology, seeks to demonstrate the role of "personal agency beliefs" in his understanding of motivation towards a goal. Ford describes personal agency beliefs as evaluations of whether one has the personal skill and the responsive environment to function effectively. These perspectives of one's self, these "evaluations," help determine what one is able to do to reach a particular goal. When a man establishes a goal of losing 10 pounds by summertime, he automatically begins to evaluate his abilities ("Do I have the discipline to do this?" or "What exercises can I realistically do to reach this goal?") and his environment ("Will my wife support me?" or "Do my eating habits make it easier or harder to reach my goal?"). Personal agency beliefs, as components in human motivation, are seminal to our daily behavior whether the goal is physical or spiritual development.

This is consistent with the purpose of Motivational Systems Theory, which is described as "a clear, coherent, and useful theory that could guide the efforts of scholars, professionals, and students concerned about, and interested in learning how to better address, real-world problems with strong motivational underpinnings" (p. ix). The "real-world" problem addressed in this study is the lack of spiritual growth among believers. Ford's theory can help our efforts to provide a more effective means for understanding spiritual growth.

This study seeks to adapt Ford's theory to the motivational aspect of the biblical notion of sanctification. The adaptation of Ford's "personal agency beliefs" seems both compatible with Scripture and useful as a theory to help clarify aspects of sanctification. Thus, this chapter of the study will argue that, for the purpose of becoming more like Christ (i.e. the goal), personal agency beliefs are

compatible with Scripture and can be helpful in our understanding of sanctificational growth.

Overview of Ford's Theory of Motivation

Within the study of human motivation, interest centers upon three phenomena, according to Ford. First, motivation includes behavioral direction that determines where people are headed and what they are trying to do as a result.
Second, motivation includes behavioral stimulation that contributes to how people are invigorated or disheartened in their functioning. Third, motivation includes behavioral regulation that governs how people decide to attempt something, persevere in it, or quit (pp. 2–3).

To address each of these phenomena, Ford incorporates three motivational
elements into a model that characterizes motivation as "the organized patterning
of an individual's personal goals, emotional arousal processes, and personal
agency beliefs." These three motivational component processes can be described
as follows:

1. Goals or Directive Cognitive Processes: "psychological processes
   that are anticipatory and evaluative in character—that is, they represent desired future states and outcomes and prepare the person to try
   to produce those desired futures" (p. 73).
2. Personal Agency Beliefs: "cognitions that are both anticipatory and
   evaluative in character;" capability beliefs are "evaluative expectancies about whether one has personal capabilities needed to attain the
   goal specified by the directive process" and context beliefs are
   "evaluative expectancies about whether the persons context will facilitate or support the person's goal-attainment efforts" (p. 74).
3. Emotional Arousal Processes: emotions "provide the person with
   evaluative information about problems and opportunities of potential
   personal relevance and help prepare the person to deal with these
   problems and opportunities" (p. 75).

Ford states that "motivation provides a uniquely valuable way of describing the integrated patterning of a set of intimately related processes" (p.
78). He therefore defines motivation as "the organized patterning of an individual's personal goals, emotions, and personal agency beliefs" (p. 78). He explains
further:

> [M]otivation is an integrative construct representing the direction a person is
> going, the emotional energy and affective experience supporting or inhibiting
> movement in that direction, and the expectancies a person has about whether
> they can ultimately reach their destination. (p. 78)

But simply having these components in place is insufficient for effective
functioning; they must interact with each other, functioning as an "interdepend-
ent 'triumvirate'" (p. 78). "Goals, emotions, and personal agency beliefs depend

on each other in ways that are so fundamental that the relevance, potency, and very existence of each process depend on the others" (p. 82).

Ford describes motivation as a psychological, future-oriented (anticipatory), and evaluative (rather than instrumental) phenomenon to distinguish motivational processes from nonmotivational processes. It is psychological because motivational processes are qualities of the person rather than properties of the context; that is, motivation resides within the person rather than in the context of the person. It is future-oriented because "motivational processes help people imagine or predict future events and consequences that are relevant and meaningful to them, thereby preparing them to ct or react in ways intended to produce futures and avoid undesired futures" (pp. 72–73). It is also evaluative because motivational processes are not instrumental in character; that is, "motivational processes identify and 'size up' problems and opportunities, but they are not responsible for solving those problems or turning those opportunities into reality" (p. 73).

Thus, with these defining elements in place, Ford describes motivation in his model as the "organized patterning of an individual's personal goals, emotional arousal processes, and personal agency beliefs." He demonstrates the interaction of these components using this formula:

$$\text{Motivation} = \text{Goals} \times \text{Emotions} \times \text{Personal Agency Beliefs}$$

Personal Agency Belief

Of the three motivational components in Ford's model, personal agency belief is the prime psychological component for this study. This component was chosen because it helps explain the necessity of evaluating one's personal capabilities and context in order for motivation to occur. The assessment of one's personal capabilities and supportive contexts provides a salient ingredient for achieving a goal. It seems that this component is also necessary for the goal of sanctificational growth. However the personal agency beliefs related to sanctificational growth would of necessity be spiritual in nature. I will test the fit of personal agency beliefs with Paul's instructions regarding sanctification in Romans 6:1-14 in the next chapter. I also hope to demonstrate that the "union with Christ" concept fits with Ford's concept of personal agency beliefs.

Goals and Personal Agency Beliefs

According to Ford, goals "play a leadership role in motivational patterns by defining their content and direction" (p. 249). Since goals must be in place before one can understand personal agency beliefs, the discussion of personal agency beliefs begins with some considerations regarding their relationship to goals.

To help explain personal agency beliefs and their relationship to goals, Ford presents the following considerations. First, personal agency beliefs are evaluative thoughts involving a comparison between a desired consequence (some goal) and an anticipated consequence (what the person expects to happen if that goal is pursued). This principle highlights the necessity of activating a goal that is of value to the person. If there is no relevant goal in place, one's personal agency beliefs have no motivational impact. For example, if a young student is certain she has the ability to earn a Master's degree (capability belief) and anticipates that she would need to move to new location to do so (context belief), but has no interest in obtaining the degree (personal goal), those beliefs will be of little significance in her life. Thus, "personal agency beliefs only matter if there is some goal in place" (p. 125).

Second, according to Ford, "the motivational burden tends to shift from goals to personal agency beliefs and emotions once a commitment has been made to pursue a goal" (p. 250). The student committed to earning a Master's degree must also evaluate her own capabilities and future context to determine if she can accomplish the goal. As the goal is pursued, her emotions will regulate and energize her activities.

Third, the temporal proximity of the goals being evaluated influences the strength or weakness of personal capability beliefs and environmental responsiveness beliefs. With proximal subgoals in place (i.e., goals that can be reached with a "manageable degree of effort"), a reasonably high degree of motivation can be maintained (i.e., beliefs generate confidence) even when the ultimate outcome remains doubtful. This seems to be Ford's explanation of the need to set smaller incremental goals that can be accomplished in order for the larger goal to be achieved. For example, if the goal is a Master's degree, the student needs to establish the goal of fulfilling each assignment in each course in order to pass the courses necessary to obtain the degree. The degree may seem too great a goal. But completing each course requirement is manageable.

Examination of Personal Agency Beliefs

According to Ford, there are two kinds of personal agency beliefs.

1. Capability beliefs: evaluations of whether one has the personal *skill* needed to function effectively (e.g., "Am I capable of achieving this goal? Do I have what it takes to accomplish this goal?").
2. Context beliefs: evaluations of whether one has the *responsive environment* needed to support effective functioning ("Does my context afford the opportunity to try to achieve my goal?" "Will my context make it easier or harder for me to attain my goal?" "Can I trust this context to support me or cooperate with me in what I try to do, or will I be ignored/rejected/ attacked?").

So, personal agency beliefs are the "psychological snapshots" that are taken when any kind of opportunity presents itself to an individual and the individual commits to achieving that opportunity. The picture of how I see myself or my circumstance relative to the challenge before me helps determine whether I am motivated or not to face that challenge. This would apply to any episode in life from getting up in the morning (e.g., "I'm too sick to go to work," or "It's too cold in the room so I'll just stay under these warm blankets") to studying for an exam (e.g., "I'm no good at algebra, so why try?" or "I know this stuff cold so this test should be easy"). Whether the goal is rearing children, writing a book, learning to drive, or playing golf, the mind is constantly evaluating one's capabilities and one's environment thus, influencing one's motivation to achieve the goal.

These considerations also help our understanding of personal agency beliefs.

1. Personal agency beliefs are often more fundamental than the actual skills and circumstances they represent. They can motivate people to create opportunities and acquire capabilities they do not yet possess. However, positive beliefs alone are not sufficient to achieve a goal but must always be accompanied by relevant skills and a responsive environment.

2. Personal agency beliefs play a crucial role in situations involving challenging but attainable goals. Possessing strong capability beliefs and positive context beliefs in the midst of a seemingly impossible situation carries strong motivational relevance to goal accomplishment because this kind of assessment "opens the door" to other "possibilities and pathways that are neither impossible nor trivially easy to negotiate" (p. 124).

3. The precise capability belief will vary depending on the particular kind of capability represented in that belief. For example, a different capability belief is needed when considering an athletic feat versus coping with a stressful situation.

4. The precise context belief will vary depending on the kind of environmental unresponsiveness represented in that belief. The environment must be congruent with the individual's "agenda" of personal goals and the person's biological, transactional, or cognitive capabilities. It must also have the material or informational resources needed to facilitate goal attainment. Lastly, the environment must provide an emotional climate that supports and facilitates effective functioning. For example, different context belief is involved when a dedicated Christian student is considers the pursuit of a PhD in education at "secular" Stanford University verses "Christian" Biola University.

Personal agency beliefs are evaluative thoughts involving a comparison between desired consequence (i.e., goal) and an anticipated consequence (i.e., what the person expects to happen if they pursue that goal). These elements of motivation interact with each other forming patterns that clarify how personal agency beliefs function.

Personal Agency Belief Patterns

Believing that motivational theories that focus on personal agency beliefs tend to obscure the degree to which capability and context beliefs jointly contribute to effective functioning, Ford has developed a taxonomy representing the different patterns of capability and context beliefs. He introduces this helpful patterning "designed to capture the essential qualities of 10 conceptually distinguishable personal agency belief patterns. This 3 X 3 heuristic scheme is summarized [in Figure 1] along with brief definitions of each of the concept labels used to summarize the 10 patterns" (p. 133).

Figure 1   The MST Taxonomy of Personal Agency Belief Patterns

CONTEXT BELIEFS		CAPABILITY BELIEFS		
		Strong	Moderate or Variable	Weak
	Positive	R	M	F
		Robust Pattern	Modest Pattern	Fragile Pattern
	Neutral or Variable	T	V	S
		Tenacious Pattern	Vulnerable Pattern	Self-Doubting Pattern
	Negative	A1 or A2	D	H
		Accepting or Antagonistic Pattern	Discouraged Pattern	Hopeless Pattern

Definitions (adapted from Webster's Seventh New Collegiate Dictionary):

R Pattern	Robust – "strong and firm in purpose or outlook"
M Pattern	Modest – "placing a moderate estimate on one's abilities"
F Pattern	Fragile – "intact but easily broken or damaged"
T Pattern	Tenacious – "suggests strength in dealing with challenges and obstacles"
V Pattern	Vulnerable – "functioning adequately but may be at risk under conditions of stress"
S Pattern	Self-doubting – "having a lack of faith in one's chances for success"
A1 Pattern	Accepting – "to endure difficulties quietly and with courage"
A2 Pattern	Antagonistic – "tending toward actively expressed annoyance or hostility
D Pattern	Discouraged – "being deprived of but potentially maintaining some confidence or hope"
H Pattern	Hopeless – "having no expectation of success"

Relative to this chart, no single personal agency belief pattern is best for all circumstances. Different personal agency belief patterns will be adaptive in different kinds of behavior episodes. Additionally, personal agency belief patterns are not necessarily stable or consistent qualities of people, but represent thoughts about personal and environmental resources that may vary across situations and change over time.

Motivation

Since personal agency belief is a component within Ford's motivation model called Motivational Systems Theory, it will be helpful to present a brief introduction to his conceptual framework. Motivational Systems Theory is derived from D. Ford's Living Systems Framework described as a "comprehensive theory of human functioning and development that is designed to represent all of the component processes of the person and how they are organized in complex patterns of unitary functioning in variable environments" (p. 245).

Ford claims that by anchoring Motivational Systems Theory in this framework, it is "possible to describe how motivational processes interact with biological, environmental, and nonmotivational psychological and behavioral processes to produce effective or ineffective functioning in the person as a whole" (p. 245).

His theory "attempts to bring coherence to the field by providing clear, precise, and comprehensive conceptualization of the basic substance and organization of motivational patterns" (p. 244). Ford claims that among the various theories of motivation, Motivational Systems Theory "provides the most comprehensive integrative conceptual framework for understanding and influencing human motivation that is presently available" (p. 173).

A foundational premise to Ford's understanding of motivation is that a person always functions as a unit in coordination with the environments in which the individual is functioning. The basic unit of functioning is termed the behavior episode which is a context-specific, goal-directed pattern of behavior that unfolds over time until a goal a) is met or met well enough, b) is preempted by another goal, or c) is evaluated as unattainable. There are four major prerequisites for effective functioning:

1. The person must have the motivation needed to initiate and maintain activity until the goal directing the episode is attained.
2. The person must have the skill needed to construct and execute a pattern of activity that will produce the desired consequence.
3. The person's biological structure and functioning must be able to support the operation of the motivation and skill components.

4. The person must have the cooperation of a responsive environment that will facilitate, or at least not excessively impede, progress toward the goal.

If any one of these components is missing or inadequate, achievements will be limited and competence development will be thwarted.

For the purposes of this study, certain observations need to be made regarding personal agency beliefs and their relationship to motivation. Ford claims that though goals play a leadership role in motivational patterns by defining their content and direction, the motivational burden tends to shift from goals to personal agency beliefs and emotions once a commitment has been made to pursue a goal. For example, the student who commits to graduating in the top 1% of his class (i.e., the goal) sets in motion a series of evaluations of his capabilities (i.e., "Do I have the intelligence and discipline to do this?") and environment (i.e., "Do I have the support and resources to do this?"). These beliefs, however, must be energized and regulated by emotion. One's emotions will influence one's behavior leading to the fulfillment, abandonment, or adjustment of the goal.

Emotions

Ford stresses the importance of emotions and their integration with goals and personal agency beliefs.

> In short, emotions are not simply motivational "add-ons" or "afterthoughts"— they are major influences in the initiation and shaping of goals and personal agency belief patterns that may seem relatively ephemeral or labile at the level of specific behavior episodes, but that in fact may be every bit as influential as cognitive processes in terms of enduring motivational patterns. (p. 147)

Within Ford's motivational theory, "emotions are motivational components that are themselves complexly organized patterns of several processes" (p. 138) consisting of three integrated subcomponents.

1. An affective (neural-psychological) component – the general subjective feeling part of the emotion; helps reveal the degree of success, failure, or problems a person is experiencing – or anticipates experiencing – in the pursuit of personal goals.
2. A physiological component – a supporting pattern of biological processing; helps produce the energy needed for effective functioning.
3. A transactional component – a pattern of motor and communicative actions designed to facilitate goal attainment; e.g., emotions can be sometimes initiated by engaging in the motor activity characteristic of a particular emotion (e.g., forcing a smile or praying and singing as in Paul and Silas's case (Acts 16:25)).

According to Ford, for emotions to have motivational meaning or personal significance, they must be related to a goal. He writes:

> The subjective experience of an emotion reveals the degree of success, failure, or problems a person is experiencing—or anticipates experiencing—in the pur-

suit of currently active personal goals. Therefore, as with personal agency beliefs, emotions that are not anchored to a goal that is currently directing or influencing the individual's activity (i.e., an intention or a current concern) will generally have little behavioral meaning or personal significance. (p. 140)

He claims that emotions also help people deal with varying circumstances by a) regulating peoples' interaction with their environment, b) energizing peoples' actions designed to produce a desired outcome.

Some emotions serve to regulate the initiation, continuation, repetition, or termination of behavior episodes (e.g., excitement and satisfaction). Others help people regulate their efforts to cope with potentially disrupting or damaging circumstances that arise during an episode (e.g., fear and anger). . . . Thus emotions help people deal with varying circumstances by providing evaluative information about the person's interactions with the environment (affective regulatory function) and by supporting and facilitating action designed to produce desired consequences (energizing function). Emotions provide a very potent mechanism for regulating behavior because affective experience has an immediacy to it that is hard to ignore . . . and because emotional states are sufficiently flexible and generic that they can be linked to almost any conceivable context. On the other hand, because emotions are usually triggered by evaluative thoughts, they can be heavily influenced by cognitive regulatory processes. (p. 51)

Emotions that function in a regulatory and energizing capacity can be seen in relationship to the development of one's character. Monitoring one's emotions can play a role in one's spiritual growth. Willard (2002) even claims that a person's emotional state of mind (e.g., "fear of," "hope for," "joy in") contributes to character formation. He writes that "healthy feelings, properly ordered among themselves, are essential to the good life. So if we are to be formed in Christlikeness, we must take good care of our feelings and not just let them happen" (p. 121).

He also mentions the significance of emotions related to motivation. He states, "We know, for example, that feelings *move* us, and that *we enjoy being moved*. They give us a sense of being alive. Without feeling we have no interest in things, no inclination to action" (p. 121). The function of emotions, described both by Ford and Willard, includes their ability to regulate one's relationship to a particular context (e.g., worship or trial) or energize one's actions toward sanctificational growth (e.g., prayer or giving).

Prominent among the emotions mentioned by Paul, are the emotions related to joy and peace. Willard (2002) states that these emotions "are *not* mere feelings, but conditions of the whole person that are accompanied by characteristic positive feelings" (p. 128).

Joy, according to Dunn (1988b) is not to be conceived as merely a "frothy feeling of delight, but as the confidence of God which can be sustained even in persecution (Matt 5:12; Rom 5:3–5; 2 Cor 7:4; 1 Thess 1:6; 1 Pt 1:6)" (p. 823). Ford's explanation of emotions as a "complexly organized patterns of processes" comprised of affective, physiological, and transactional components seems to fit the various forms of "joy" in the New Testament. Theologian Erich Beyreuther (1976) provides an overview of the word.

There are three main groups of words in the NT which denote human joy and happiness and express its special character. In the case of *chairo* physical comfort and well-being are the basis of joy. Hence [there is] the use of the v[er]b in the good wishes which people express on greeting one another and on parting. They refer to the benefits of health and happiness which, in fact, people wish for themselves. On the other hand, *euphraino* indicates the subjective feeling of joy, and *agalliaomai* the outward demonstration of joy and pride and the exultation experienced in public worship. (p. 352)

Evaluating one's degree of joy, whether a sense of well-being or feeling, while engaged in a goal-oriented activity will influence one's motivation toward the goal. Joy can be one emotional factor that energizes the activity or regulates its continuance.

Scripture also indicates the emotion and quality of peace as significant in spiritual development. For example, Philippians 4:7 ("And the peace of God which surpasses all understanding will guard your hearts and your minds in Christ Jesus") points to the emotion of peace as guardian of "heart and mind." Greek language scholar Gerald Hawthorne (1983), comments:

Paul seems here to be referring to the tranquility of God's own eternal being (Caird), the peace which God himself has (Barth), the calm serenity that characterizes his very nature . . . and which grateful trusting Christians are welcome to share. If they do, then not only will inner strife resulting from worry cease, but external strife resulting from disagreements among Christians has the potential of coming to an end as well. (p. 184)

Experiencing serenity, in the context of external strife, provides an opportunity for peace to regulate and energize relationships with others. Conversely, inward turmoil may indicate an anxiety related to one's desire for a cooperative environment (or any goal) and one's activities in reaching the goal of peace (or any goal). Thus, Paul concludes his letter to the Ephesians with the salutation, "Peace be to the brothers, and love with faith, from God the Father and the Lord Jesus Christ" (Eph 6:23). New Testament scholar Harold Hoehner (2002) comments that peace denotes "well-being" in both an internal and external environment: "It not only expresses objective peace but also a subjective feeling of well-being. In the present context "peace" refers to the peace that comes from God, but indeed, peace of God within believers should produce peace between believers" (p. 873).

Emotions are essential to progressive sanctificational growth. Willard (2002) writes:

Understanding of the role of feelings in life and in the process of spiritual formation is absolutely essential if that process is to succeed as it should. There are many ways we can go wrong with reference to feelings. They are extremely influential on all that we are and do—much more so than they should be for our own good, and mainly because we accord them greater significance than they deserve.

They more than any other component of our nature, are the "trigger" of sinful action . . . Feelings have a crucial role in life, but they must not be taken as a *basis* for action or character change. That role falls to insight, understanding, and conviction of truth, which will always be appropriately accompanied by feelings . . . We must understand how love, joy, and peace can be our portion in every state of life and can lead us into a radiant eternity with God. (pp. 138–139)

How then are emotions developed and changed for spiritual growth? Willard claims that people cannot change emotions "head-on," nor resist them or redirect them by "willpower." A better strategy is "that of *not having* them [the feelings]—of simply changing or replacing them" (p. 118). Instead of giving in to feelings,

the person who happily lets God be God does have a place to stand in dealing with feelings . . . They have the resources to do what they don't want to do and to not do what they want. They know and deeply accept the fact that their feelings, of whatever kind, do not have to be fulfilled. . . . And with respect to feelings that are inherently injurious and wrong, their strategy is not one of resisting them in the moment of choice but of living in such a way that they do not have such feelings at all, or at least do not have them in a degree that makes it hard to decide against them when appropriate. (pp. 118–119)

Reasoning will influence emotion if one is willing to be influenced. Willard explains:

Feelings can be successfully 'reasoned with,' can be corrected by reality, only in those (whether oneself or others) who have the habit and are given the grace of *listening* to reason even when they are expressing violent feelings or are in the grip of them. (pp. 124–125)

Feelings must also be controlled.

Self-control is the steady capacity to direct yourself to accomplish what you have chosen or decided to do and be, even though you "don't feel like it." Self-control means that you, with steady hand, do what you *don't* want to do (or what you want *not* to do) when that is needed and do *not* do what you want to do (what you "feel like" doing) when that is needed. In people without rock-solid character, feeling is a deadly enemy of self-control and will always subvert it. The mongoose of a disciplined will under God and good is the only match for the cobra of feeling. (p. 127)

The ability of human beings to participate in emotional change is introduced in this discussion. Reasoning and self-control under the direction of God are derived from one's character. In other words, it is from a transformed character that believers have the ability to control, change, and discipline themselves to become people who properly use emotions for good. In this process, one finds the proper place of the emotional component in motivation which is necessary in striving towards the goal of sanctificational growth.

Comparable Concept in Bandura's Self-Efficacy Theory

Personal agency belief theory, among all motivational theories, shares the greatest conceptual commonality with Albert Bandura's self-efficacy theory. This is most notably true with the concepts of capability beliefs and "self-efficacy expectations." In this section, I will compare and contrast the two theories to give us a better understanding of Ford's theory and to demonstrate the strength of Ford's theory.

Ford wrote *Motivating Humans* with the purpose of providing the reader with "a coherent, unified description of the basic substance of human motivation" (p. 2). He accomplishes this goal by "organizing the major theories and theorists around categories of motivational processes rather than assuming a linear presentation of each of these theories" (p. 2). Thus, the book "emphasizes the need to integrate separate but generally compatible ideas into a systematic understanding of what motivation is and how it operates" (p. 2).

In chapter six, Ford does provide a comprehensive survey of 32 motivation theories. These include theories that have developed over the years in a variety of fields of study, prominent contemporary theories, "grand" psychological theories that dominated the field in the early part of the century, and classic theories of work motivation.

Among these theories, a few—Social Learning Theory (Rotter), Learned Helplessness/Hopelessness/Optimism Theory (Seligman), and Self-Efficacy/Social Cognitive Theory (Bandura)—include aspects of what Ford calls personal agency beliefs. The most prominent theorist, Albert Bandura, has generated a body of work developing the concept of self-efficacy and its role in impacting behavior.

"Belief in one's ability to exert control over one's surroundings is central to the concept of self-efficacy described by Bandura (1977, 1982)" (Geen, 1995, p. 124). The theory grew from the context of clinical therapy but "now applies more generally to goal-related behavior" (Geen, p. 124). This development can be seen from an early example of empirical research in which Bandura (1977b) hypothesized that "expectations of personal efficacy determine whether coping behavior will be initiated, how much effort will be expended, and how long it will be sustained in the face of obstacles and aversive experiences" (p. 191). Bandura's theory focuses upon a) self-efficacy expectancies (beliefs about personal capabilities that may vary according to the difficulty of performance accomplishment, b) generality (range of contexts represented), and c) strength (vulnerability to disconfirming information).

Later, in a 1982 article he addresses the centrality of the self-efficacy mechanism in human agency, by stating that "self-percepts of efficacy influence thought patterns, actions, and emotional arousal" (p. 122), thus expanding the concept beyond coping with difficult situations.

Psychological changes are, therefore, mediated through cognitive processes, "but the cognitive events are induced and altered most readily by experiences of mastery arising from successful performance" (Bandura, 1977a, p. 79). Bandura continues:

> Psychological procedures, whatever their form, alter expectations of personal efficacy. Within this analysis, efficacy and outcome expectations are distinguished . . . An outcome expectancy is defined here as a person's estimate that a given behavior will lead to certain outcomes. An efficacy expectation is the conviction that one can successfully execute the behavior required to produce the outcomes. Outcome and efficacy expectations are differentiated because individuals can come to believe that a particular course of action will produce certain outcomes, but question whether they can perform those actions. (p. 79)

From this brief presentation, one can observe the similarities between Bandura's self-efficacy concept and Ford's capability belief concept primarily. Both theories focus on the role of personal capabilities within a context. Additionally, Bandura and Schunk (1981) and Bandura (1989) have integrated the concept of goal setting into their theoretical structure which is common to both theories. However, Ford believes Bandura fails "to address goal content issues in a serious way" (p. 85).

A difference in the two theories lies in the emphasis upon the context. Whereas Ford gives equal status to the motivational contributions of capability and context beliefs, Bandura (1982) gives precedence to self-efficacy over context beliefs, or what he terms, "outcome beliefs" (p. 140).

Ford also believes his capability beliefs model "affords greater theoretical scope and precision" (p. 128) than does Bandura's self-efficacy model.

> First, because "skill" is defined . . . as the entire set of nonmotivational psychological processes, i.e., capability beliefs can reflect confidence or doubts about any number of personal strengths or weaknesses: perceptual, motor or communicative skills; memory or information-processing capabilities; self-control or self-regulatory skills; capabilities for dealing with stressful circumstances; or one's capacity for selective or sustained attentional or activity arousal. (p. 128)

Therefore, when people say they are unable to do something, they may be referring to different kinds of skill deficits in different circumstances. "Bandura's failure to clarify the different kinds of skills that may be involved in self-efficacy judgments is one reason his theory has generated a fair amount of confusion and controversy in recent years" (p. 128), writes Ford.

Second, according to Ford, Bandura's concept of self-efficacy judgments has usually been restricted to beliefs about *task* goals in context-specific behavior episodes while Ford's concept of capability beliefs may pertain to any kind of goal (e.g., affective or social relationship goals) and any level of abstraction (p. 129).

Thus, it seems that Ford's personal agency belief theory provides a more comprehensive and precise understanding of capability and context beliefs than does Bandura's self-efficacy beliefs at least in light of Ford's purposes for developing his theory. Ford is attempting to provide, through a heuristic process of integrating models, a coherent whole, i.e., the entire (motivational) pie, while Bandura is seeking to present only a slice of the motivation process.

Personal Agency Beliefs and Christian Worldview

How well does Ford's concept of personal agency belief fit with a Christian worldview? In the following discussion, issues of compatibility will be examined. I will present a claim made by Ford regarding personal agency beliefs and then illustrate or provide an example of its applicability within a biblical or Christian context. Though various aspects of Ford's theory of motivation have been introduced, this exercise will only include the salient concepts and principles pertaining to personal agency beliefs.

Ford describes personal agency beliefs as "evaluative thoughts involving a comparison between a desired outcome (i.e., some goal) and an anticipated consequence (i.e., what the person expects to happen if they pursue that goal" (p. 251). The two kinds of personal agency beliefs, capability (i.e., skills) and context (i.e., responsive environment) can be observed in biblical literature as well.

Goals in Scripture could be equated with the desire to obey certain commands or exhortations such as pray, submit, love, walk, care, grow, turn, resist, rejoice, follow, live, think, listen, give, serve, and believe. Reaching these goals has spiritual and practical consequences. Believers must now determine if they have the ability to accomplish these goals by evaluating their personal capabilities and the responsiveness of their present environment. Usually, these commands are accompanied by a statement of ability or supportive environ which must be believed in order for the goal to be accomplished.

For example, James writes, "'God opposes the proud but gives grace to the humble.' Submit yourselves therefore to God" (4:6–7). Commenting on this verse, Moo (2000) states that God is "merciful, gracious, all-loving, and willingly supplies all that we need to meet his all-encompassing demands" (p. 191). God's grace finds a home in those capable of humbling themselves. Moo continues, "God's gift of sustaining grace is enjoyed only by those willing to admit their need and accept the gift" (p. 191). Submission is possible due to the grace God provides. Thus, "If God gives the grace to meet his claim on our lives to those who are humble, then we must become humble if we expect to enjoy that grace" (p. 192). This call to humility and submission (vv. 7, 10) encompasses the commands of vv. 7–9 (i.e., subgoals) that are essential for the accomplishment of the goal of a genuine relationship with God and among believers (4:1–2, 11–12). When people see themselves as humbly submitted to God, they are capable of living in the power of God's grace which brings graciousness to all relationships.

When applied to other commands to be obeyed, personal agency beliefs seem to play an essential role in motivating the believer towards the goal of becoming more like Christ in sanctificational growth. This notion seems compatible with Ford's claim that it is not enough to have a goal in mind and the objective skills and environment needed to attain it. But people "must also *believe* that they have the capabilities and opportunities needed to achieve their goal" (p. 124). These kinds of beliefs often prove more fundamental to goal accomplishment than the actual skills and circumstances they represent. Thus, such beliefs can motivate people to create opportunities and acquire capabilities they do not yet possess (p. 124).

A practical application of this notion within a Christian worldview could be the understanding that since God created humans in his image—including personality, self-transcendence, intelligence, morality, gregariousness, and creativity (Sire, 1997, p. 27)—Christians can believe that they have the capacity to improve themselves. Sire (1997) states another tenet of Christian theism that is applicable to the aforementioned claim.

> Human beings were created good, but through the Fall the image of God became defaced, though not so ruined as not to be capable of restoration; through the work of Christ, God redeemed humanity and began the process of restoring people to goodness, though any given person may choose to reject that redemption. (p. 32)

Redeemed ones have the resources "to create opportunities and acquire capabilities they do not yet possess" through the work of Christ and the Holy Spirit.

Ford also explains that personal agency beliefs play a crucial role in situations involving challenging but attainable goals. (i.e., goals that are neither impossible nor trivially easy to accomplish). This notion highlights the role of broader personal agency beliefs, such as confidence, hope, and optimism, related to certain kinds of goals. These beliefs "play a crucial role in situations that are of greatest developmental significance – those involving challenging but attainable goals" (p. 124). So these beliefs become key targets of intervention for parents, teachers, counselors or others interested in helping people function effectively.

It may be possible to apply this notion of personal agency beliefs being crucial to accomplishing challenging but attainable goals in sanctificational development. Paul wrote his second letter to the Corinthians, a church divided and in error, to admonish and instruct them in their relationship with God and with each other. As he ends the letter he places some goals before them. "Finally, brothers, rejoice. Aim for restoration, comfort one another, agree with one another, live in peace, and the God of love and peace will be with you...The grace of the Lord Jesus Christ and the love of God and the fellowship of the Holy Spirit be with you all" (2 Cor 13:11–14). Yet, he also prays that they will experience the grace of Jesus Christ, the love of God, and the fellowship of the Spirit as they seek to accomplish these goals. Believing that in relationship to the triune God these qualities are available and can also be manifested, provides the motivation for believers to seek to live such a life.

A notion pertaining specifically to capability belief is stated as: "The precise meaning of a capability belief will vary depending on the particular kind of capability represented in that belief" (p. 251). For example, the capability beliefs needed to throw a football are different than the capability beliefs needed to struggle with aging. This principle may also be supported and illustrated from

Scripture. Belief related to the Christian's capability to behave in such a way as to not offend another Christian (1 Cor 8:1–13) is different than the kind of belief needed to endure affliction (2 Cor 4:7–18).

In 1 Peter 1:13–21, the believer's ability for holy conduct is addressed (vv. 15–16) by focusing on the particular kinds of skills that enable such conduct.

> [P]reparing your minds for action, and being sober-minded, set your hope fully on the grace that will be brought to you at the revelation of Jesus Christ. As obedient children, do not be conformed to the passions of your former ignorance, but as he who called you is holy, you also be holy in all your conduct. (vv.13–16).

Bible professor Peter Davids' (1990) comments on this passage support the principles of personal agency belief already mentioned as well as the current capability belief discussion. He states that believers are to "set their hope fully" not "comparing qualities of hope (total versus less than total) but objects of hope" (i.e., on the return of Christ vs. the transitory and corrupt of earthly life) (p. 65). He continues:

> Their hope is to be in the "grace" that the revelation of Jesus Christ will bring to them. . . . Yet Peter is not suggesting a flight into dreams of the future . . . but rather a careful evaluation of present behavior in the light of future goals and an unseen reality. Therefore the way one hopes "totally" is by "getting your minds ready for work" and being "well-balanced." (p. 65–66)

There seems to be a connection between the goal of "hope" that comes in thinking about Christ's return and the resulting behavior or certain kinds of "skills" such as mind readiness and balance that nurtures the hope. In other words, hope is demonstrated by a ready mind that is prepared for action and is well-balanced (i.e., "complete clarity of mind and its resulting good judgment" (Davids, 1990, p. 66)) versus becoming despondent due to various trials (v. 6). "Their hope, however, is not a 'pie-in-the-sky-by-and-by' type of hope isolated from the present world and its concerns, but one that directly controls how they live in the present" (Davids, 1990, p. 67). This sets the context for holy living presented in verses 14–16. The beliefs related to the skills needed to cultivate this kind of hope is different than the beliefs related to the kinds of skills needed to demonstrate, for example, Christlikeness in marriage (Eph 5:22–33).

Ford's final principle pertaining to personal agency belief is specific to context beliefs. "The precise meaning of a context belief will vary depending on the kind of environmental unresponsiveness represented in that belief" (p. 251). For example, a couple planning a vacation may have good reasons, positive emotions, and strong capability beliefs to have a great holiday but may choose to forego the vacation if they anticipate bad weather conditions, vehicle failure, lack of support by one of the spouses, or restrictions from the place they want to visit. In this case, the environment is seen as untrustworthy or uncooperative so the trip is canceled (p. 130).

The context for sanctificational growth would include such "environmental" components as the Holy Spirit, the church, creation, or spiritual friendships. In this case, the environment would be considered supportive and helpful for spiritual growth. However, one could also perceive the environmental components that are also mentioned in Scripture such as Satan, sin, the world system, the flesh or an unwise/ungodly advisor each of whom would be non-supportive in nature. In these cases, the environment could be considered as untrustworthy or uncooperative and so spiritual growth is inhibited. The Christian who desires spiritual growth but perceives the spiritual environment as dominated by these untrustworthy components rather than the supportive ones (e.g., Holy Spirit, being "in Christ," Scripture, church community), will struggle or fail in sanctificational growth.

Additionally, when the environment is not favorable or supportive, an understanding Ford's taxonomy of personal agency belief patterns comes into play. Note in Table 1 that when the context beliefs are "neutral or variable" or "negative," in order for motivation to take place, people can draw from capability beliefs that are "strong." If this does not happen, they may become vulnerable, discouraged, or hopeless (with weak capability beliefs). However, when people evaluate their own capabilities as strong in spite of an unsupportive context, then a "tenacity" pattern is evidenced that will "deal with challenges and obstacles." (p. 134). Ford describes the tenacious pattern as "high in motivational potency because it, too, leads to effortful persistence in challenging or stressful circumstances" (p. 135). So, even though the context is unsupportive, success can be experienced if capability beliefs are strong ("It's not going to be easy, but I can reach my goal if I keep at it and don't let the [criticism/hassles/losses] get to me") (p. 135). This can be applied to personal and spiritual challenges.

In contrast, for an optimally responsive environment, different functional elements are needed according to Ford (pp. 130–133). These include (with application from a Christian worldview) the following principles.

1. The environment must be compatible with an individual's "agenda" of personal goals (e.g., "Do my friends, family, work associates, or church leaders support my goal of becoming like Christ?").
2. The environment must be compatible with the person's biological, transactional, or cognitive capabilities (e.g., "Can I comprehend basic doctrinal truths?").
3. The environment must have the material or informational resources needed to facilitate goal attainment (e.g., "Do I have access to sacred and other writings that inform and aid the transformation of my mind towards Christian formation?").
4. The environment must provide an emotional climate that supports and facilitates effective functioning (e.g., "Am I receiving the loving encouragement that supports me as I attempt to reach my goal?").

There seems to be an ease to the integration of Ford's personal agency belief principles with certain theological concepts. This fits one of the methods of integration proposed by Moreland and Craig: "Theology fills out and adds details to general principles in another discipline and vice versa, and theology helps one practically apply principles in another discipline and vice versa" (2003, p. 21). For our purposes, in chapter five we will examine the interaction of personal agency beliefs with the theological concepts represented in Romans 6:1–14 seeking to fill out and add details to the personal agency belief principles since Ford does not possess a Christian perspective nor present a distinctively Christian theory.

In analyzing the compatibility of personal agency beliefs with certain biblical concepts, Ford's model, perhaps due to its comprehensive and integrative nature emphasizing the common elements and themes of motivational theories, provides a flexible and broad model that accommodates pertinent theological and biblical ideas. By design, Ford's basic theory was developed to interact with other specialized theories of motivation, which could include motivational notions related to sanctification. In other words, it provides a "macro-theory" allowing other more specialized theories to fit into it resulting in a robust theory and practical principles that can be applied to other issues of concern. Generally speaking, Ford's model facilitates the goal of this study in helping to address the motivational issues inherent in sanctificational growth.

Review and Preview of Issues Being Addressed

I have examined the place of human effort and God's effort in the synergistic work of sanctificational growth (chapter two). Included in this work of sanctification is an acknowledgement that believers have some responsibility for their own spiritual growth primarily through forming beliefs and making choices from a transforming character (chapter three). In this chapter, I discussed a particular type of belief, called personal agency belief, which complements other components of sanctificational growth. This chapter introduced Ford's theory of motivation including personal agency beliefs, demonstrating the compatibility of his theory with theological and biblical ideas. I also sought to demonstrate how people can understand and engage their personal capability and context beliefs as a component of motivation in sanctificational growth.

In the next chapter I examine the believer's "union with Christ" and examine the fit of this doctrine with Ford's personal agency belief model and Willard's VIM model. I argue that the Christians' belief in their union and identification with Christ provides a vital link in the process of sanctificational growth and that these two models provide heuristic patterns for the understanding of this process.

CHAPTER 5

AN EXAMINATION OF THE BELIEVER'S UNION WITH CHRIST INTEGRATED WITH FORD'S PERSONAL AGENCY BELIEFS MODEL AND WILLARD'S VIM MODEL

Of the six chapters in this dissertation this one is the most crucial since it takes the components of sanctificational growth already discussed and integrates them so a more comprehensive understanding of progressive sanctification can be formulated. How are believers capable of sanctificational growth? The response to this question indicates the structure one's understanding of sanctification will take. Some elements that contribute to one's doctrine of sanctification have been introduced. These elements have been presented under the umbrella of "human participation" (chapter two) as evidence that human beings have been created and redeemed by God so that they are able to grow in his likeness through the process of sanctification.

As has been discussed, much in Scripture is devoted to encouraging believers to grow in Christlikeness (chapters one and two). Additionally, humans have been created with capabilities that can be used for sanctificational growth (chapter three). One of these capabilities is the power to assess one's personal skills and environment to determine if a particular goal can be accomplished (chapter four). In this chapter I will examine "personal agency beliefs" and their place as motivational components in sanctificational growth. The examination of this psychological component suggests its contribution to a comprehensive understanding of sanctificational growth.

This contribution is suggested as I integrate the theological concept of union with Christ with personal agency beliefs. I chose this concept because union with Christ seems to be a significant and essential tenet to sanctificational growth and because it seems to fit Ford's personal agency belief concept. I suggest that the integration of these two concepts provides additional substantiation for human participation in sanctificational growth and thus a more comprehensive understanding of progressive sanctification.

The discussion of the union with Christ motif is conducted primarily in dialogue with systematic theologian Bruce Demarest who represents the prevailing evangelical understanding of the concept. He has devoted a lengthy chapter in his theological work, *The Cross and Salvation* (1997, pp. 313–344) examining the believer's union with Christ compared to other evangelical theologians who provide brief analysis of the subject (Grudem, 1994, pp. 840–850; Erickson, 1996, pp. 948–954; 974–975). The discussion in this chapter begins with an analysis of the believer's union with Christ.

However, believers do not automatically mature spiritually because they are in Christ. They must appropriate this reality into their experience. In other words, if human participation includes the freedom to make choices, are there particular biblical courses of action that must be considered for sanctificational growth to occur?

This leads to an examination of the notion of intentionality related to personal transformation and sanctificational growth. The framework for this discussion is Dallas Willard's VIM model of personal transformation. I suggest that this model provides a heuristic pattern explaining Paul's instruction in Romans 6:1–14 and the process of sanctificational growth from this passage. If VIM describes a process of transformation, there may be a particular biblical pattern found in Scripture that fits or supports that process.

I argue that believers are able and required to think of themselves in union with Christ as dead to sin and alive to God, accepting this into their belief system (i.e., worldview) and thus intentionally contributing to their sanctificational growth. According to Dallas Willard (1988), believers are responsible to "consciously and purposefully regard" themselves as "dead to sin and alive to God in union with Jesus Christ" (p. 115). This claim is examined exegetically and practically by testing the fit of VIM with Paul's instructions. Thus, this chapter ends with an examination of the transformational potential of the union with Christ concept as presented in Romans 6:1–14.

Conceptual Context: A Summary of Chapter 2–4 Claims

The primary claim for this dissertation is that believers are capable and responsible to participate in God's work of producing spiritual growth. Thus, I have examined key components of human participation within sanctification for the purpose of better understanding the process of growth in Christlikeness or holy living.

Chapter one introduced the theological concept of sanctification that forms the backdrop for the whole discussion. It also introduced the notion of intention as found in Willard's VIM model. For the purposes of this study, intention is examined as entailed in free will and in human participation especially as these concepts contribute to progressive sanctification.

In chapter two the claim was made that believers participate in sanctificational synergism. Though my purpose was not to determine the level of divine and human participation in sanctification, I suggested that human participation is necessary at some level. Sanctificational synergism, as I am using the descriptive term, includes divine and human participation in the progressive aspect of sanctification.

Chapter three centered on the claim that believers are able to participate in the sanctificational process due to their free will. The freedom to make decisions, however, is made related to one's character. One's character was discussed as a set of beliefs and desires which were examined as contributors to character formation and sanctificational growth. Belief was seen as a component to one's view of reality or worldview. These elements interact for sanctificational growth to occur.

In chapter four the claim was made that believers participate by viewing themselves through their personal agency beliefs which contribute to motivation for sanctificational growth. Personal agency beliefs are evaluative thoughts regarding one's capabilities and one's context for goal–oriented action. How believers view themselves and what they believe about their spiritual state or condition affects their sanctificational growth.

Believer's Union with Christ

Many references in the New Testament present the concept of the believer's union with Christ (John 15:4–5; 1 Cor 1:4–5, 15:22; 2 Cor 5:17; Eph 1:3–4, 2:10; 1 Thess 4:16; Col 1:27; Gal 2:20). Being in union with Christ suggests a frame of reference in which believers can view themselves and their environment as supportive of sanctificational growth. In other words, since Christians are incorporated into Christ, they have the spiritual ability and context required for sanctificational growth. Therefore, a study of the believer's union with Christ should contribute to a comprehensive understanding of sanctification both positional and experiential.

Rationale

There are reasons for discussing the believer's union with Christ in relationship to sanctification and human participation in sanctification. The rationale for including the concept of union with Christ in the discussion of sanctificational growth focuses on 1) its foundational nature, 2) its results and provisions, and 3) its connection to the other conceptual components of this study.

The theological discussion of union with Christ provides a conceptual foundation for understanding its implications for sanctificational growth. As theologian Millard Erickson (1985) states, "it is clear that our continued walk in the Christian life, our sanctification, is dependent on union with him" (p. 974). Demarest (1997) also believes that union with Christ is "a central verity, indeed a touchstone reality of the Christian life and experience" (p. 313).

Not only does this union seem foundational to the Christian experience, there are those who suggest that it is also at the heart of Paul's experience of Christ and his view of the spiritual life. Michael Gorman (2001), professor of New Testament and early church history, suggests that "the notion of being 'in Christ' lies at the heart of Pauline spirituality" (p. 35). Others (Schweitzer, 1931; Sanders, 1977) suggest that "participation in Christ" is the center of Paul's theology rather than justification by faith.

David Rightmore (1996), Professor of Bible and Theology, agrees:

> The heart of Pauline theology is union with Christ. . . . Although often overlooked in favor of an emphasis on justification by faith, Paul's treatment of the spiritual life in Christ is central to the apostle's understanding of religious experience. . . . Union with Christ is organically related to both justification and sanctification (Rom. 5:8–10), and as such, life "in Christ" is the essence of Paul's proclamation and experience. (p. 789)

The agreement regarding the foundational nature of the union concept among these theologians suggests that an understanding of the believer's union with Christ is essential to their ability to live a sanctified life. It also suggests that union with Christ deserves consideration in this discussion of sanctificational growth.

Lastly, with the inclusion of the union with Christ concept with the other concepts presented in this study, a more complete portrayal of sanctification is possible. Though I will focus on the two models of personal agency beliefs and VIM, these models provide case studies for human participation which include free will, belief formation, and character formation. Implicit to the discussion is the integration of these essential components of human participation and thus sanctificational growth.

Introduction

The concept of union with Christ is expressed in the New Testament as Christ in the believer (John 15:5; Gal 2:20; Col 1:27) and the believer in Christ (John 15:5; 1 Cor 15:22; 2 Cor 5:17). Demarest (1997, pp. 314–326), provides a historical survey of interpretations of union with Christ pointing out that because this doctrine is a "somewhat enigmatic concept" it has been interpreted in different ways in the history of the church. Union with Christ has been interpreted as 1) ontological (Neoplatonists and Mystical theologians), 2) sacramental (Roman Catholics, Lutherans, Anglo–Catholics), 3) covenantal (Reformed and Covenant theologians), 4) moral or filial (Socinians, Rationalists, Liberals), and 5) experiential. Demarest describes this union as a "discrete stage in the *ordo salutis*" which is regarded as a "profound relation of personal identification and fellowship with the Savior" (p. 323). He suggests that this view "most faithfully coheres with the biblical point of view" (p. 326). I will focus on the fifth or "experiential" interpretation.

Theologian J. I. Packer (1994) also supports this final view as he describes union with Christ as a) identification with Christ— "a relation to *Jesus' person—*one of *discipleship*" and b) incorporation into Christ – the Christ–event that describes the reality of the believer's actual death and resurrection, living and reigning with Jesus and through Jesus appropriated by faith (p. 119). The dual aspects of union as identification and incorporation in their relationship with Ford's personal agency beliefs of capability and context will be examined later in this chapter.

Descriptive Pauline Terminology

Paul uses a variety of phrases to describe the believer's union with Christ. Taken as a whole, they provide a means of explaining this intimate relationship of Christ and Christian which proves to be essential to our understanding of sanctificational growth and to the doctrine of sanctification.

"The *en Christō* and related expressions found in the Pauline writings do not embody a single idea but are elastic phrases that embrace a wide range of meanings" (Demarest, 1997, p. 326). Its versatility is seen in the following discussion framed by Catholic theologian, Joseph Fitzmyer (1967), who notes that four prepositional phrases express the incorporation of Christ and Christians "suggesting different facets of Christ's influence on the life of the Christian" (p. 68).

1. The preposition *dia* or "'through' normally expresses the mediation of Christ in a statement of which the subject is the Father." (e.g., 1 Thess 4:14; "For since we believe that Jesus died and rose again, even so, *through Jesus*, God will bring with him those who have fallen asleep.")

   "Through" can be used "of immediate agency, causation, instrumentality" and translated "by means of" or "by" as in John 1:3 ("all things were made by/through [*dia*] him") (Mounce, 1993, p. 136). (Jn 1:7, 10; Rom 1:5; 5:1, 10; 2 Cor 5:18; Gal 4:7; Eph 1:5; 1 Thess 5:9).

2. The preposition *eis* or "into" as in the phrase "into Christ" or "into the name of Christ" is usually used with baptism (i.e., "baptized into Christ") or with belief (i.e., "believe in Christ") and denotes the movement to incorporation and so may be translated "to," "toward" or "unto." This usage is found in Romans 6:3 in the question, "Do you not know that all of us who have been baptized into Christ Jesus were baptized into his death?" It is also used in 2 Corinthians 1:21 ("it is God who establishes us with you in (*eis*) Christ"), Ephesians 4:15 ("your faith in (*eis*) the Lord Jesus"), and Colossians 2:5 ("the firmness of your faith in (*eis*) Christ")

   To illustrate even the elasticity of this usage, Donald Guthrie, New Testament scholar, comments that Romans 6:3 "seems to mean that baptism inaugurated us into a condition in which we now become "in Christ." In this case there is no essential distinction between the two expressions ["in Christ" and "into Christ"] with regard to new life in Christ" (1981, p. 656).

3. The preposition *syn* or "with" is used with the object "Christ" but also is compounded with verbs and adjectives and can in these constructions express a double relationship of the Christian to Christ. Thus, it either suggests the identification of the Christian with the preeminently redemptive acts of Christ's historical and risen life [e.g., "suffer with," "be crucified with," "buried with," or "raised with"] or the association of the Christian with Christ in eschatological glory [e.g., "to be with Christ"] (p. 69).

This preposition can refer then to the beginning (i.e., identification) as well as the ongoing association with Christ even throughout eternity. This is the usage found in Romans 6:4 ("buried with him"), 6:5 ("united with him"), 6:6 ("crucified with him"), and 6:8 ("died with Christ," "live with him"). Because *syn* is often a prefix to the verb, it expresses a "co-" aspect of the intimate identity with Christ such as "co–burial," "co–united," or "co–crucified." It denotes that Christ's action was the believer's action as well.

4. The preposition *en* or "in" with the object Christ (or "Lord" or "him") "occurs 165 times in Paul's letters" and is most commonly used "to express the close union of Christ and the Christian, an inclusion or incorporation that connotes a symbiosis of the two" (pp. 69–70).

In this usage, *en Christō* ("in Christ") describes the personal union of the believer or believers with Jesus Christ. Paul referred to Christ being in the believer individually (Gal 2:20), collectively (Rom 8:10; 2 Cor 13:5; Col 1:27), and corporately (1 Cor 15:22). "So intimate is the union between Christ and the believer (or believers) that the apostle regarded Christ in the believer and the believer in Christ as virtually equivalent expressions" (Demarest, 1997, p. 327). For Paul, being "in Christ" is similar to having "Christ in me" (Gal. 2:19–20).

Paul also illustrated the incorporation of the Christian and Christ using the symbolism of a building (Eph 2:19–22), a temple (1 Cor 3:16–17), a human body (Rom 12:4–5; 1 Cor 12:12–27; Eph 1:22–23; 4:4, 12, 15–16; 5:23, 30), and marriage (Eph 5:23–32). Demarest (1997) provides this conclusion for the use of these illustrations:

> The preceding relational images suggest that "in Christ" should be understood in a subjective or experiential sense; the data does not allow us to limit the "in Christ" motif strictly to the formal or objective meaning of the believer's new situation in the state of salvation. (p. 329)

Gorman (2001) provides another explanation of incorporation by proposing that Paul's language suggests a relationship that is not so much mystical as it is spatial: "to live within a 'sphere' of influence" (p. 36). He continues:

> The precise meaning of the phrase varies from context to context, but *to be "in Christ" principally means to be under the influence of Christ's power, especially the power to be conformed to him and his cross, by participation in the life of the community that acknowledges his lordship.* (p. 36)

This discussion demonstrates the broad range of meanings regarding the phrases related to the believer's union with Christ. Yet there is enough evidence from Paul's writing to conclude that to be "in Christ" is an essential component in our understanding of the Christian life as well as foundational to our understanding of sanctificational growth and the doctrine of sanctification. It seems that the heart of a theology of sanctification is the believer's union with Christ which has practical implications for growth in sanctification.

The Nature of Union with Christ

According to Demarest (1997, pp. 330–333), biblical revelation describes the nature of the believer's identification or union with Christ. He summarizes the nature of union with Christ with the following statements about which I elaborate:

1. As a supernatural union rather than a natural union. Jesus spoke concerning the Father and himself, "we will come to him and make our home with him" (John 14:23) since God the Father and God the Son are one (John 10:30). God's permanent indwelling of the believer is also mentioned in 1 John 4:12 and 16. The thought seems to be that believers experience the immediate presence of the Diety (Morris, 1995, p. 581).

2. As a spiritual union since Christ indwells believers (or the community) by the Holy Spirit. To the disciples, Jesus promised the Holy Spirit (John 14:16–17) who would "be with" them, "live with" them, and "be in" them. Believers are joined to Christ and become "one spirit with him" (1 Cor 6:16–17) and become the dwelling place for the Holy Spirit (1 Cor 6:19), that is, their bodies become God's temple in which the Spirit lives (1 Cor 3:16–17). This indwelling of the Spirit is true not only individually but also corporately (Eph 2:21–22). The believer's union with Christ is brought about by Holy Spirit baptism (1 Cor 12:13, cf. Rom 6:3–4). Thus, Paul can say that Christ indwells believers (Rom 8:10) and that the Spirit indwells believers (Rom 8:9, 11).

3. As an organic union, meaning that "it has an organization similar in complexity to that of living things, i.e., the "body of Christ"— "Christ, the Christian, and all other Christians are united under the metaphor of the human body" with believers as "members" of the body and Christ as the "Head" and "source of its unified life" (pp. 331–332). Union is described using the metaphor of the human body with its members who belong to one another (Rom 12:5, 1 Cor 6:15; 12:12–27; Eph 1:22–23; 4:12–16; 5:23, 30–32) with Christ as the head (Eph 4:15–16; Col 2:19).

4. As a vital union involving a new quality of life. "Since Christ himself is the source and repository of life (John 1:4; 5:26; 11:25; 14:6; 1 John 5:20), those who are related to him by faith participate experientially in his supernatural life" (p. 332). John wrote, "God gave us eternal life, and this life is in his Son. Whoever has the Son has life; whoever does not have the Son of God does not have life" (1 John 5:11–12). Those in Christ possess eternal life, now and forever (John 3:15–16, 36; 1 John 5:13). Paul gave testimony of the Christian's

new supernatural life in Christ declaring, "Christ lives in me" (Gal 2:20).

5. As a comprehensive union since "[t]he Christian's entire life and actions are exercised in relation to Christ—his life, values, power, and rule" (p. 332). Scripture indicates that being in Christ provides resources enabling the believer to display Christ's likeness in speech (Rom 9:1), work (1 Cor 15:58), and proclamation of truth (2 Cor 2:17). Abiding in Christ empowers believers to bear the spiritual fruit of Christlikeness (John 15:1–17; Gal 5:22–25).

6. As a mysterious union since the mutual interpenetration of Christ and the believer which cannot be completely understood. Believers are limited in their ability to fully comprehend the statements from the New Testament (primarily Paul and John) explaining the believer's union with Christ, the believer's oneness in Christ, and the believer's indwelling by Diety. Of Christ's oneness relationship to believers, Paul writes, "This mystery is profound, and I am saying that it refers to Christ and the church" (Eph 5:32). Paul describes as "mystery" God's revelation of the church and its glory which is "Christ in you" (Col 1:24–29).

The nature of the believer's union with Christ individually and corporately is multi–faceted and mysterious. Yet, the New Testament is clear that believers are identified with and incorporated into Jesus Christ. The need when applied to progressive sanctification is to not only know about the nature of union with Christ but to experience it beginning with regeneration.

Basis and Results

Scripture suggests that Christ's death and resurrection provides the basis for the believer's union with Christ.

Scripture uniformly testifies that the basis or ground of union with Christ is the Savior's atoning death and resurrection. The apostle Paul stated that identification with Christ in his death ("I have been crucified with Christ") and participation in his supernatural life ("Christ lives in me") is made possible by "the Son of God, who loved me and gave himself for me" (Gal 2:20). (Demarest, 1997, p. 329)

Paul states his individual identification with Christ made possible by Christ's death and resurrection in Galatians 2:20. Yet there is also a corporate aspect to this identification and participation in Christ's death and resurrection. In Romans 6:3 Paul asks, "Do you not know that all of us who have been baptized into Christ Jesus were baptized into his death?" This question emphasizes a corporate aspect of the death of Christ. When Christ died on the cross, "all of us" who would be incorporated into him by faith also died or are "at once identified with a death that has already happened" (Guthrie, 1981, p. 645).

The Apostle Paul continues in Romans 6:4 to state that just as Christ was raised from the dead, believers now walk "in newness of life." The corporate aspect of the risen life is seen here as well. When Christ was raised from the dead, believers were in some sense raised with him so that they could walk in newness of life. The corporate sense of the resurrection is seen in Colossians 3:1 ("If then you (2nd person, plural) have been raised with Christ") and continuing, "For you have died, and your life is hidden with Christ in God. When Christ who is our life appears, then you also will appear with him in glory" (Col 3:3–4).

Thus, the believer's union with Christ, grounded in his death and resurrection, results in the believer's own death and resurrection. Demarest writes, "Paul expounded these spiritual outcomes by reference to major historical events in the experience of Jesus and by the phrase 'with' (*syn*) Christ, which occurs a dozen times in the Pauline letters" (p. 333). The use of "with Christ" (see p. 82) is most prominent in Romans 6 which distinguishes the outcomes of the believer's union with Christ.

1. The Christian has been crucified and has died with Christ. Paul wrote that believers "have been united with him like this in his death" (Rom 6:5) and "our old self was crucified with him" (Rom 6:6). Since Christ's crucifixion was a historical event, the incorporation of believers in that death was also historical (Guthrie, 1981, p. 645). Believers are considered as having been crucified with Christ when he was crucified. Believers have "died with him" (2 Tim 2:11) meaning that they have died "together with" Christ. ("It is agreed that this *suv–* has Christ in view" (Knight, 1992, p. 403)). The aorist indicative "is used in a 1st class cond[itional] cl[ause]which assumes the cond[ition] as a reality" (Rogers and Rogers, 1998, p. 502). Paul also writes, "For you have died, and your life is hidden with Christ in God" (Col 3:3).

2. The Christian has beTen buried with Christ. Paul wrote, "We were-therefore buried with him through baptism into death" (Rom 6:4). "Buried with," the translation of *synetaphamen* meaning "to bury together," indicates the corporate nature of this union with Christ's burial. "The significance of the burial imagery is personal death to sin's domination and a complete breach with the old way of life" (Demarest, 1997, p. 334).

3. The Christian has been made alive with Christ. As Christ was raised from the dead, believers have new life in union with him (Rom 6:4). Paul wrote, "God, who is rich in mercy, made us alive with Christ even when we were dead in transgressions" (Eph 2:4b–5). New life is indicated in statements such as, "And you, who were dead in your trespasses and the uncircumcision of your flesh, God made alive together with him" (Col 3:13) and "we will also live with him" (2 Tim 2:11). Through faith in Christ at conversion, believers move from a condition of spiritual death to a state of unending, spiritual life (Demarest, 1997, p. 335).

4. The Christian has been resurrected with Christ. Paul writes that in baptism believers have also been "raised with him through your faith

in the power of God, who raised him from the dead" (Col 2:12). "Raised with him" can refer to "being raised up with from death, physical or spiritual" and in this case, "of participating in the resurrection of Jesus" (Danker, 2000, p. 967) just as in Colossians 3:1 ("If then you have been raised with Christ") where the conditional clause assumes present reality and the aorist indicates completed action. Baptism, therefore, seems to picture the resurrection of believers corporately and individually based on Christ's resurrection.

5. The Christian will be glorified with Christ. Paul wrote, "When Christ, who is your life appears, then you also will appear with him in glory (Col 3:4; cf 1:27b). "Glorification includes the future resurrection of the Christian's physical body (Rom 6:5b, 8:11; 1 Cor 15:22b; 1 Thess 4:16), the enjoyment of everlasting life in heaven (1 Thess 4:17b), and participation in Christ's heavenly rule (Rom 8:17)" (Demarest, 1997, p. 335).

In union with Christ, God has "blessed us in Christ with every spiritual blessing in the heavenly places" (Eph 1:3) and is able to meet every need (Phil 4:19). Additionally, there is a completeness for believers in their union with Christ, "For in him [Christ] the whole fullness of the dwells bodily, and you have been filled in him, who is the head of all rule and authority" (Col 3:9, 10). In Christ believers find their spiritual needs met.

The above listing of the results of the believer's union with Christ indicates the connection of this doctrine with Romans 6:1–14 which contains, explicitly or implicitly, all of the "with Christ" outcomes mentioned above. This passage will prove significant in our understanding of union.

Union with Christ and Sanctification

The following discussion indicates that since believers are united with Christ, they also possess the holiness of Christ. That is, Jesus Christ, as the believers' sanctification (1 Cor 1:30) and in whom they live, provides both the position of holiness and the power for holiness. It follows then, that experiential sanctification emanates from union with Christ.

Scripture supports a relationship between union with Christ and sanctification. Paul describes the church in Corinth as "those sanctified in Christ Jesus, called to be saints [holy]" (1 Cor 1:2). The use of the perfect participle for the word sanctified "indicates a completed action with results continuing into the present" (Mounce, 1993, p. 272). The designation of the Christian community in Corinth as sanctified emphasizes their present state or condition once placed in Christ Jesus. By being placed in Christ by the Holy Spirit they are now considered holy. Furthermore, that they are "called to be saints" denotes a core disposition demonstrated in actions characteristic of saints. The present participle "called" emphasizes the continual and habitual actions which are to characterize their lives. Thus, both aspects of sanctification, positional and experiential, are suggested in this verse and are related to being "in Christ."

First Corinthians 6:17–20 presents the connection between union with Christ and experiential sanctification: "But he who is joined to the Lord becomes one in spirit with him. Flee from sexual immorality. . . . Or do you not know that your body is a temple of the Holy Spirit within you, whom you have from God? You are not your own for you were bought with a price. So glorify God in your body." New Testament scholar Gordon Fee (1987) comments:

> In light of vv. 19–20, Paul probably is referring to the work of the Spirit, whereby through the "one Spirit" the believer's "spirit" has been joined indissolubly with Christ. The believer is united to the Lord and thereby has become one S/spirit with him. . . . [Thus] he argues that sexual immorality in particular is a sin against one's own body, which is "for the Lord" because it is also a "temple of the Spirit." (pp. 260–261)

A holy life, which here is characterized by separation from sexual immorality and is designated by the Holy Spirit's indwelling, is possible due to the Christian's being united to the Lord by the Spirit. This understanding of sanctification is consistent with Paul's statements in 1 Thessalonians 4:4–9 where separation from sexual immorality coincides with his instructions to please God in holiness.

The connection of union with Christ and sanctification can also be seen in the Apostle John's statement in 1 John 2:5b–6: "By this we may be sure that we are in him: whoever says he abides in him ought to walk in the same way in which he walked." Believers are designated as being "in him," a statement of incorporation and position, which demonstrates itself in conduct reflective of Christ's conduct. I. Howard Marshall (1978), professor of New Testament, proposes that "in him" is a phrase "synonymous with "Live [literally, abide] in him" in verse 6. He writes, "Being in him and living in him are to be regarded as synonyms, the latter word perhaps emphasizing the permanence of the relationship and the need for perseverance on the part of men" (p. 127). Colin Kruse (2000), New Testament expert, elaborates.

> [W]hen the author speaks about living in God, as he does here in 2:6, or of being in God, as he does in 2:5b, it is something more than keeping God's commands that he has in mind. It is the new and very real spiritual existence that believers enjoy, and which is effected through the agency of the Spirit, who bears witness to the truth. (p. 81)

This passage supports the idea that union with Christ, or in this case God, provides the basis for the believer to walk as Christ walked in an intimate relationship with the Father, by the Spirit, obedient to God's will.

Each of these passages connects union with Christ with sanctification. The believer's incorporation and identification with Christ, the "in-Christ" motif, provides the basis for sanctificational growth.

Union with Christ and the Holy Spirit

The ability of believers to grow in sanctification has its theological foundation in their identity and incorporation with Christ as discussed in the previous section. Within that discussion, however, is the acknowledgement that this union is effected by the Holy Spirit. There seems to be a direct association between the believer's union with Christ and their relationship with the Holy Spirit. Conversely, there seems to be an alliance between the concepts of Christ being in the believer and the Holy Spirit's presence in the believer.

In the discussion regarding sanctification (chapter one) and above, it was noted that the Holy Spirit plays a crucial role in sanctificational growth. Again, there seems to be a relationship between the place of believers in Christ and the work of the Spirit to make this "in–Christ" existence a practical reality. In other words, the believer's experiential holiness may be due to "the present experience of the risen Christ indwelling the believer's heart by the Spirit" (Rightmore, 1996, p. 789).

This relationship between the indwelling Spirit and indwelling Christ can be seen in John's record of Jesus' words to his disciples. The Holy Spirit is described by Jesus as "another Advocate" (John 14:16) (cf., Jesus as Advocate in 1 John 2:1) and as "the Spirit of truth" (John 14:17) (cf., Jesus as truth in John 14:6) drawing positive comparisons to Jesus' relationship with his disciples and the Spirit's relationship with them after his departure (John 14:16). In the context of the Spirit's coming, Jesus states that "[i]n that day you will know that I am in my Father, and you in me, and I in you" (John 14:20). The Holy Spirit's presence in them is associated with Jesus being in them. Furthermore, the Holy Spirit is the one the Father sends "in Jesus' name" (John 14:26) perhaps meaning because Jesus himself asks the Father or because the Spirit will continue the work of Christ (i.e. "in his place") (Morris, 1995, pp. 582–583). The Holy Spirit will indwell Christ's disciples as he himself would indwell them.

The Apostle Paul explicitly relates the Holy Spirit to the believer's union with Christ in Romans 8:1–2, "There is therefore now no condemnation for those who are in Christ Jesus. For the law of the Spirit of life has set you free in Christ Jesus from the law of sin and death." Those "in Christ Jesus" (twice) are not condemned by the law of sin and death because they possess the Spirit of life who sets them free from this law. The Spirit of God is also referred to as the Spirit of Christ (Rom 8:9). Indeed, "we note in Romans 8 that the Spirit (vv. 5–6, 9a, 11b), the Spirit of God (v. 9b, 11a), the Spirit of Christ (v. 9c), and Christ (v. 9d, 10) are all used interchangeably" (Demarest, 1997, p. 331). Paul also relates Christ's indwelling with the Spirit's indwelling, "But if Christ is in you, although the body is dead because of sin, the Spirit is life because of righteousness" (8:10). "It is clear that the believer who by faith has come to be joined with Christ . . . has not only Christ but also the Spirit resident in them. The indwelling Spirit and the indwelling Christ are distinguishable but inseparable" (Moo, 1996, p. 491).

In addition, the Holy Spirit is the divine agent of incorporating believers into the body of Christ (1 Cor 12:13). Christ is one body (12:11) which is perhaps a reference to the church (i.e., "the body of Christ," cf. 12:27–28). There-fore, ("for") believers have been "baptized in" and "caused to drink" one Spirit, who creates one body.

The believer's life in Christ is in reality life in the Spirit. Paul identifies the believer's relationship to God as one of "adoption" as sons in Galatians 4:6. Corresponding to this adoption is the placement of the Holy Spirit, "the Spirit of his Son," into the heart of every "son." Paul's portrayal of the Spirit as the "Spirit of his Son" fits the context and indicates that not only has God given believers the status of "sons" but has also provided the presence and power of his Son in their lives. The same Spirit who indwelt Jesus now indwells these believers. They can, therefore, live as sons calling God "Abba/Father" and mani-festing their status as heirs of God (vv. 6b–7) as Jesus did (Mark 14:26).

Christ lives in believers by the Holy Spirit. "Christ's presence is directly connected to the eschatological gift of the Spirit. In Christ, the Spirit is at work carrying out God's redemptive purposes" (Rightmore, 1996, p. 791). He summa-rizes:

> For Paul to be "in Christ" was to be "in the Spirit." Paul distinguishes between Christ and the Spirit, but views the function of the latter as mediating the for-mer to believers. As the operative agent of God in the Christian's life, the Spirit never acts apart from Christ. Thus, although distinct entities, Christ and the Spirit are experienced together, and are the means by which persons come into relation with God. (p. 792).

Romans 6:1–14 is a key passage in portraying the union with Christ concept as a significant component in sanctificational growth. If union with Christ is possible only through the indwelling Spirit, why is there no mention of the Holy Spirit related to the union with Christ concept and sanctificational growth in this passage? Gordon Fee argues for the Spirit's implicit inclusion in the passage.

Fee (1994) believes that the Holy Spirit is involved in the descriptions of Romans 6:1–14. He writes, "even though the Spirit is not expressly mentioned in this text, there can be little question that lying behind the language is the life of the Spirit" (p. 502). He points out several examples in linguistic correspon-dences of concepts in 6:1–14 and the Spirit.

1. "walk in newness of life" (6:4) is "echoed of the Spirit in 7:6 (in *newness* of *Spirit*), 8:2 (the *Spirit* of *life* = the Spirit who gives life), and 8:4 (who *walk* according to the *Spirit*)" (p. 499).
2. The new life of righteousness related to union with Christ (6:5–11) is "conjoined in 8:10–11 through the Spirit of Christ" (p. 500).
3. Regarding sin and the body, "in 6:12–14 he speaks about sin reigning in our mortal bodies, language picked up in slightly different form in 8:13: 'by the Spirit put to death the deeds of the body'" (p. 500).

Thus, to Fee (1994) this passage can only be explained by Paul's Trinitarian view of life in the present age. He claims: 1) "The key to righteousness for Paul is to be found in the work of both Christ and the Spirit" (p. 500), 2) "God's sav-ing work is brought about through Christ and the Spirit—Christ effects it; the Spirit appropriates it to the life of the believer" (p. 501) and 3) "Whereas Paul firmly distinguishes between the work of Christ and that of the Spirit, he just as surely sees the work of each to be about the same thing overall—God's redeeming a people for his name" (p. 501). He continues:

> From both perspectives, that of Christ and that of the Spirit, the same result is effected. Christ's death and resurrection free the believer from sin; the Spirit's indwelling frees the believer from sin. The work of Christ is obviously the central reality, ever and always for Paul; but without the work of the Spirit that of Christ goes for naught. (p. 501)

Fee's arguments are helpful in understanding the relationship of Christ's indwelling and the Spirit's indwelling, either of which may be implicit in these passages. He also reminds the student that Paul's teaching about the gospel includes sanctification (chapters 6–8) initiated by union with Christ providing freedom from the dominion of sin (chapter 6) and the law (chapter 7) and lived in the Spirit (chapter 8). Such help is needed to keep in balance the divine–human elements in sanctification.

Integration of Union with Christ and Two Models of Human Participation

With the theological context in place, I now move to the integration of the "union with Christ" concept with Ford's personal agency belief model and Willard's VIM model to see if there is a fit. These models provide a reasonable limit to the theological and exegetical dimensions of the union with Christ discussion. It is beyond the scope of this work to provide detailed theological analysis or Scriptural exegesis especially as it relates to Romans 6. Adequate analysis of Scriptures that relate to Willard's VIM model and Ford's personal agency model is provided. The resources used for this analysis include both primary and secondary sources.

These models also provide examples of human participation in sanctificational growth. In the following discussion the primary phrase used to describe the intimate relationship with Christ is "union with Christ." However, it may be used interchangeably with phrases such as "in Christ," or "with Christ."

Conceptual Integration of Union with Christ With Personal Agency Beliefs

A practical understanding of the concept of union with Christ may result from viewing it in relationship to the concept of personal agency beliefs. It appears that the "union with Christ" concept entails the concepts of capability and context as described in Ford's theory. Thus, the personal agency belief model may act as a heuristic tool to better understand union with Christ and its appropriation into the Christian's experience. This exercise also serves as an opportunity to integrate the two concepts in direct interaction that may mutually reinforce each concept.

I argue in this section that the Christians' belief regarding their union with Christ provides a personal agency belief that affects the motivational aspect of sanctificational growth. The lack or distortion of this particular belief leaves the believer without a necessary realized context and capability to function in holiness or sanctification. But with an understanding or "consideration" of one's union with Christ comes an ability to grow spiritually towards Christlikeness. Theologian Wayne Grudem (1994) states that because Christ is in "continuing possession of all the spiritual resources" needed to live the Christian life, and because "every spiritual blessing was earned by him and belongs to him," then those who are in union with him have access to these resources and blessings. In other words, "these blessings are ours" and therefore, we can live a new life in Christ (p. 843).

In chapter four I reviewed Martin Ford's (1992) theory of personal agency beliefs. He describes them as "evaluative thoughts involving a comparison between a desired consequence (i.e., some goal) and an anticipated consequence (i.e., what the person expects to happen if they pursue the goal)" (p. 251). There are two kinds of personal agency beliefs:1) capability beliefs, and 2) context beliefs.

For this study, the "desired consequence" or goal is sanctificational growth. Evaluating the "anticipated consequences" that is, what must happen in pursuing this goal, is the primary subject of this dissertation. To effectively pursue sanctificational growth, believers must participate in the process utilizing their free will through a transformed character while realizing they are part of God's work of sanctification. I suggest that one aspect of participation is the evaluation of one's capabilities and contexts entailed in one's union with Christ leading to sanctificational growth.

Capability Beliefs

Capability beliefs can be described as cognitive evaluations of one's skills or capacities to function effectively. Ford (1992) characterizes "skills" as "the entire set of nonmotivational psychological processes" (p. 128). Therefore, "capability beliefs can reflect confidence or doubts about any of a number of personal strengths or weaknesses" such as self–control or self–regulatory skills, capabilities for handling stressful situations, or the capacity to choose or maintain an activity (p. 128). Capability beliefs are one's judgments regarding one's capacity to mobilize personal or acquired resources to accomplish a specific goal. In other words, the believer may ask, "Am I capable of becoming more spiritually mature?" or "Do I have what it takes to grow spiritually?"

Based upon the theological understanding of the believer's union with Christ developed earlier in this chapter, Christians are capable of living sanctified lives due to the inherent provisions entailed in their union with Christ including the power of the Holy Spirit.

First, there are multiple spiritual resources innate and available in union with Christ. Theologian Sinclair Ferguson (1988) uses the analogy of deposit and withdrawal to describe these available resources and their use.

We can only draw on resources which have already been deposited in our name in the bank. But the whole of Christ's life, death, resurrection and exaltation have, by God's gracious design, provided the living deposit of his sanctified life, from which all our needs can be supplied. Because of our fellowship (union) with him we come to share his resources. (p. 50)

According to the Apostle Paul, Christians "have been given fullness in Christ, who is the head over every power and authority" (Col 2:10). "Fullness in Christ" may indicate that believers possess "completeness" in union with Christ since the word accentuates the fullness of persons with "powers" or "qualities" (Danker, 2000, p. 828) that are, in this case, entailed in their union with Christ. These qualities could include life, righteousness, faithfulness, wisdom, goodness, and love that are available in every believer to be appropriated into their lives. Thus, believers live in a state of completeness in Christ with "unrestricted access to the divine power which will shape them, too, into the divine image (3:10)" (Dunn, 1996, p. 153). Due to the resources available in this state, Paul can confidently pray that "you may be filled with all the fullness of God" (Eph 3:19). Here is found another example of the positional (i.e., indicative) and progressive (i.e., imperative) aspects of sanctification.

An additional provision corresponds to the power of the indwelling Christ referred to in John 15. According to the Apostle John, Christians are capable of bringing forth spiritual fruit only in union with Christ: "I am the vine; you are the branches. Whoever abides in me and I in him, he it is that bears much fruit, for apart from me you can do nothing" (v. 5). Christ is the life of the vine that produces fruitfulness in prayer (v. 7), other matters (v. 8) including obedience in love (vv. 9–14, 17). The point Jesus seems to be making is that believers only bear fruit as they are "enabled by the infusion of supernatural life brought about by spiritual union with Christ, the source of new life" (Demarest, 1997, p. 341).

It is imperative, therefore, that believers actively "remain," "continue" (to live) in Christ who continues to abide in them (v. 4). As believers participate in a dynamic relationship with Jesus Christ they experience his abiding presence which produces spiritual fruit. The resources of Christ are available to all believers but are only activated as they live such lives (i.e., by abiding in him) that he will continue to abide in them. The two "abidings" cannot be separated. Abiding in Christ is the essential prerequisite of fruitfulness (Morris, 1995, p. 595).

Acknowledging that Christ abiding in the believer is tantamount to the Spirit abiding in the believer, it seems reasonable to connect John 15:1–17 to Galatians 5:16–25 with Paul's description of a fruitful life in the Spirit—a life that evidences the character of Jesus Christ. This kind of fruitfulness is only possible as Christians draw upon the powerful resources entailed in their union with Christ as illustrated by the vine. Believers indeed have "what it takes" to live a fruitful and sanctified life. They have the spiritual capabilities for sanctificational growth. The need is for believers to develop the skills to appropriate these capabilities through training themselves for godliness (1 Tim 4:7–8).

Other passages support the claim that believer's have the ability to live righteously as a result of union with Christ. In Galatians 2:19–20, Paul gives testimony of his own crucifixion with Christ ("I have been crucified with Christ") and the reality of Christ's life in him ("no longer do I live, but Christ lives in me") enabling him to live unto God not under the jurisdiction of the law or his own ego, but in the power of Christ's own life. As New Testament scholar F. F. Bruce (1982) comments:

> Those who place their faith in Christ are united with him by that faith—united so closely that his experience now becomes theirs: they share his death to the old order ('under law'; cf. 4:4) and his resurrection to new life . . . Having died with Christ in his death, the believer now lives with Christ in his life—i.e. his resurrection life. In fact, this new life in Christ is nothing less than the risen Christ living his life in the believer. The risen Christ is the operative power in the new order, as sin was in the old. (p. 144)

Paul's testimony indicates that the believer has a sufficient resource in the very life of Christ and his power in which reside the necessary capacities for sanctificational growth. However, Paul also states that Christ lives in him and "the life that I now live in the flesh I live by faith in the Son of God." It seems that the Christian appropriates the multiple resources available in Christ by believing the reality of their existence in Christ.

Professor of New Testament Richard Longenecker (1990) states the "belief" concept in terms of "focusing one's attention" on one's union with Christ which provides direction for Christian living (p. 92). Paul focuses on his "co-crucifixion" with Christ and the resultant resurrected life of Christ residing in him rather than the law or human ego in order to live for God.

In another passage, 2 Corinthians 5:17, Paul states, "if anyone is in Christ he is a new creation. The old has passed away, behold the new has come." According to Danker (2000, pp. 572–573) "creation" (*ktisis*) can mean "the result of a creative act" (i.e., "that which is created") and can refer to the creation of individual things or beings (i.e., "creature) or the sum total of everything created (i.e., "creation"). The meaning Paul intends here seems unclear. Thus, "new creation" has been debated among exegetes with three meanings surfacing. According to Biblical studies professor J. R. Levison (1993), new creation can be understood as: (1) individual converts; (2) the community of faith; or (3) the cosmos as a whole (p. 189). However, he states:

> It is not possible to choose definitely between these options. Nor is it necessary, for all three mutually illuminate each other. The convert, as part of a community of faith, enters the cosmic drama of recreation that God inaugurated at the resurrection of Jesus Christ and will bring to completion at the Parousia. (p. 190)

Biblical translations of *kainē ktisis* usually follow one of the first two distinctions. It is translated "new creation" (RSV, NRSV, ESV, NEB, REB, JB) or "new creature" (KJV, NKJV, TEV, LB, Phillips, NASB, NIV); the former supporting the dawning of a new age and the latter with the creation of a new life (Belleville, 1996, p. 154). For a thorough discussion of this debate one can read

New Creation in Paul's Letters and Thought (Hubbard, 2002) in which the author concludes that "new creation" refers to the newness of the person in Christ.

However, both meanings of "new creation" have significance to our study. When applied to the individual believer, the notion of being a "new creature" supports the Christian's capacity to live a new, sanctified life as a new person. "New creation" is in this way understood as an "alternative formulation" of the life side of the death–life equation and connected to Paul's "new birth" concept (Hubbard, 2002, pp. 233–234). From this new life the believer can actually live a new life. Richard Gaffin (1988), Professor of Biblical and Systematic Theology, upholds this notion when he writes that "the deepest motive for holy living is not gratitude for the forgiveness of sin but the determination of the believer's existence as a new creature" (p. 1546). Viewing oneself as a new creation in Christ seems to provide the perspective that one has the capability to grow spiritually. In other words, "in Christ there is a new way of 'seeing' since he has made all things new" (Martin, 1986, p. 152).

Not only have Christians become new creatures in Christ, but if the alternative meaning of "new creation" is adopted, they have also entered a new age. They have been placed into a new state or position, a new environment, in Christ. Professor of New Testament Ralph Martin (1986) explains that since the accent falls on a person (*tis* = "anyone") entering the new order in Christ, this makes the "new creation" an eschatological term for God's age of salvation. Thus, he believes Paul is talking about a "new act of creation," not an individual's renovation (p. 152). New Testament historian Paul Barnett (1997) agrees claiming that Christ has divided history into two "aeons:" the "no longer" aeon when all things were "old" and the "now" aeon when all things have become, and are, "new." He also describes this "new creation" as coterminous with the "new covenant" (3:6). Together they divide history into two epochs: the "old" things of creation and of the "old covenant" (3:14) coincide, as do the "new" things of the "new covenant" and the "new creation." (p. 298)

If this view of "new creation" is accepted, it suggests that the believer now lives in a new environment or a new "context," using Ford's term, which provides support for sanctificational growth. In other words, growth is possible because Christians have been placed in a God–bestowed (5:18) "friendly" environment in Jesus Christ providing a supportive surrounding to progress in Christlikeness. Even difficult situations can be perceived as growth producing since they take place in this environment.

Being a "new creature" as a "new creation" seems to correspond with Ford's concept of personal agency beliefs as referring to one's personal capabilities and context. Either interpretation of "new creation" fits this model of personal agency beliefs. This is, again, a recognition that Christians are capable of holy living based upon the "new" resources made available in union with Christ.

According to the doctrine of union with Christ whereby the believer is in Christ and Christ is in the believer and whereby the believer has been crucified, buried, and resurrected with Christ to newness of life, there is the possibility of growth and implied motivation for growth due to the resources God provides in this intimate relationship. Such resources as the Holy Spirit, Christ's life, and new creation "blessings," plus freedom from the "old order," the law, and death provide essential capacities for holy living.

An additional integrative conception can be developed from this discussion. Ford describes capability beliefs as "evaluations of whether one has the personal SKILL needed to function effectively" (p. 251). If "skill" is understood from an Aristotelian perspective as dispositions for excellent functioning, then such virtues as courage, honesty, truthfulness, temperance, or discipline would qualify as skills that need to be evaluated when considering a goal. These "excellences" have the potential to be developed in union with Christ and in the power of the Spirit of Christ.

There is also a biblical application. Wisdom, particularly as described in the Old Testament, can be understood as "skill." *Sophia* denotes for example, "a specialist knowledge in a particular field." But over and above this, "it is concerned quite generally with the sagacious behavior which enables a man to master life (Prov. 8:32–36)." In this sense, wisdom is conduct in obedience to the will of God and begins with the "fear of the Lord" (Goetzmann, 1978, p. 1028). Skill (i.e., "applied knowledge) in a particular field, in mastering life, or in obedience to God is the kind of wisdom that needs to be evaluated according to Ford. Theologian and Jewish scholar Louis Goldberg (1980) writes:

> The essential idea of [wisdom] represents a manner of thinking and attitude concerning life's experiences; including matters of general interest and basic morality. These concerns relate to prudence in secular affairs, skills in the arts, moral sensitivity, and experience in the ways of the Lord. . . . The emphasis of OT wisdom was that the human will, in the realm of practical matters, was to be subject to divine causes. Therefore, Hebrew wisdom was not theoretical and speculative. It was practical, based on revealed principles of right and wrong, to be lived out in daily life. (p. 282)

So, believers seeking sanctificational growth need to evaluate their living skills as wisdom capable of contributing to their growth. Motivation for growth can be cultivated as believers reverentially acknowledge God which is the beginning of wisdom (Job 28:28). For believers, "the source of all wisdom is a personal God who is holy, righteous, and just. . . . He alone must provide this wisdom for man's guidance so that man can live the best possible moral and ethical life" (Goldberg, 1980, p. 283).

Perhaps this wisdom relates to Paul's statement that God has made Christ Jesus "our wisdom and our righteousness and sanctification and redemption" (1 Cor 1:30). Wisdom here seems to be related to salvation as delineated by the terms righteousness, sanctification, and redemption. The context of this verse is God's wisdom. Fee (1987) states:

> God's wisdom—the real thing—has to do with salvation through Christ Jesus. In a community where "wisdom" was a part of a higher spirituality divorced from   ethical consequences, Paul says that God has made Christ to become "wisdom" for us all right, but that means he has made him to become for us the one who redeems from sin and leads to holiness—ethical behavior that is consonant with the gospel. (p. 87)

True wisdom is only available in relationship to God through Jesus Christ who is our wisdom "packaged" in salvation along with righteousness, sanctification, and redemption. In other words, it is in union with Christ that people have "positionally" the wisdom (i.e., "skills for living") needed for sanctificational growth. The concept of wisdom as skills for living provides a prospective component for motivation in sanctificational growth.

Each of these passages suggests that believers have the capability for sanctificational growth. Based upon the theological understanding of the believer's union with Christ developed earlier in this chapter, Christians are capable of living sanctified lives due to the inherent provisions entailed in their union with Christ including the power of the Holy Spirit.

Context Beliefs

Personal agency beliefs also entail context beliefs as evaluative thoughts regarding the responsiveness of one's environment, that is, whether it is supportive or not in the pursuit of a goal. For believers in pursuit of sanctificational growth, there are two contexts that need evaluation: a) their personal or individual context which being united with Christ provides and b) their corporate context which being in the "body of Christ" (i.e., church or Christian family and friends) provides. Each environment seems to contribute to the believer's motivation to live righteously and thus needs to be evaluated.

The first context is the personal spiritual environment entered into at regeneration and dwelt in by the believer. The Apostle Paul describes this new residency, "He has delivered us from the domain of darkness and transferred us to the kingdom of his beloved Son in whom we have redemption, the forgiveness of sins" (Col 1:13–14). God has rescued believers from the "rule" or "authority" (*exousia*) of darkness and moved them (*metestēsen*) to another place. To be "transferred" means to "remove from one place to another" and here, to be "transplanted into" the rule of Jesus Christ (Danker, 2000, p. 625). Believers now reside in the kingdom "belonging to the Son" including a new life received in Christ ("in whom") who released them from sin when he paid the price by his death on the cross. "Union with Christ thus marks the end of the old existence and the beginning of the new" (Demarest, 1997, p. 323).

Not only do believers have a new residency in Christ, they also have a new standing before God in Christ. "For our sake he [God] made him to be sin who knew no sin, so that in him we might become the righteousness of God" (2 Cor 5:21). Fulfilling God's purpose ("so that") through his Son ("in him"), believers have met God's requirement for righteousness and received his provision of justification. In Christ believers are justified, that is, they have the status of being right before God. This explains why Paul could write, "There is therefore no condemnation to those who are in Christ Jesus" (Rom 8:1).

It is also "through Christ" that the believer's spiritual condition (and status) has changed. Paul writes that "he [God] predestined us for adoption through Jesus Christ, according to the purpose of his will" (Eph 1:5). Believers are accepted by God and granted a favorable position as children of God (John 1:12) by "adoption." Believers have a new legal status as God's children and also experience being favored by God (1 John 3:1). The Spirit has a crucial role in adoption (Rom 8:12–17; Gal 4:4–7). Adoption has effects on the believer's life such as forgiveness, reconciliation, freedom along with the Father's care including parental "discipline," provisions to meet needs, love, and goodwill (Erickson, 1985, pp. 961–965). For the believer in Christ, "all things" have become new (2 Cor 5:17).

In Romans 6:3, Paul describes the believer's union with Christ using the phrase "baptized into Christ Jesus" and "baptized into his death." With the preposition "into" this baptism indicates "the sense of a movement into in order to be involved with or part of" rather than a concrete reference to the ritual of baptism (Dunn, 1988a, p. 311). This suggests that believers have been moved into Christ in order to be a part of his death. The person baptized is, as it were, buried with Christ since for Paul, to be baptized in Christ, is to be involved in Christ's death (Danker, 2000, p. 164). Having died with Christ the believer has also died to sin.

This new existence in union with Christ entails not only a personal death (v. 3) but also a personal resurrection to new life (v. 4) that is no longer enslaved to sin (vv. 6–7). Packer (1994) describes this "in–Christ" existence:

> In the Jesus to whom we go in faith the power of the whole Christ–event [union] resides, and that in saving us he not only sets us right with God, but also, so to speak, plugs us in to his own dying, rising and reigning. Thus we live in joyful fellowship with him knowing ourselves justified by faith through his death, and finding therewith freedom from sin's tyranny and foretastes of heaven on earth through the transforming power within us that his dying and rising exerts. (p.120)

The phrase "baptized into Christ Jesus" is a way of expressing the believer's incorporation into a new realm of living not only positionally but also practically. Willard (1988) explains this new "context" that allows believers to enjoy communion with Christ due to their union with him.

> What he experienced *then* we *now* also experience through our *communion* with him. . . . We participate in the new form of life . . . This new form of life provides not only new powers for our human self, but also, as we grow, a new center of organization and orientation for all of the natural impulses of our bodily self. (pp. 114–115)

It is this "new form of life" that the believer needs to evaluate when considering a commitment to sanctificational growth. When evaluated or "considered" (Rom 6:11), believers may discover that this is the actual personal context in which they live. It is the place where God has placed them in union with Christ from which they have the necessary power and support center (i.e., "a new center of organization and orientation") to live righteously. Along with this personal spiritual environment, believers also live in a corporate spiritual domain.

The second context to be evaluated is a corporate environment, that is, living in union as between Christ and "all the saints" (Eph 1:1; Phil 1:1) or the church (1 Thess 1:1; 2 Thess 1:1). Believers have been united with one another by virtue of being united in Christ and by the Holy Spirit. This corporate union is to provide essential support for believers who are intent on becoming more like Christ.

Being "in Christ" demonstrates itself in "one body" as indicated in 1 Corinthians 12:12–13. This passage suggests a corporate concept whereby all believers are admitted into the Christian community and identified with Christ himself (v. 12). Paul's message in these verses countered the divisiveness of the troubled Corinthian church. He instructed them that the church body is one even though it contains many members just as it is with Christ (v. 12). Already mentioned in 10:16 and alluded to in 11:29, the "body of Christ" must be understood as being "one" even though it has many members. "In saying 'So it is with Christ,' Paul is probably using metonymy. Thus 'Christ' means the church as a shortened form for the 'body of Christ'" (Fee, 1987, p. 603). Paul seems to be comparing the church and Christ using the corporate aspect of Christ rather than the individual person of Christ. Paul continues by explaining how the oneness of the body happens—by the one Spirit. The oneness of the Corinthians is not only due to Christ's body being one, but due to "their common experience of the Spirit" (Fee, 1987, p. 603). Believers have been brought into unity by the Spirit which makes them a member of the body of Christ.

The idea of believers being members of one body in Christ is also highlighted in Romans 12:3–8. Here the emphasis is on the function of the various members according to the gifts granted them. Verse 5 applies to our discussion most directly, "so we, though many, are one body in Christ, and individually members one of another." In Christ, each believer has been incorporated into one body and has been identified with others in that body.

Incorporation is also suggested by Galatians 3:27–29 where baptism into Christ creates a new corporate identity—"all one in Christ Jesus." Believers are therefore no longer primarily identified by social, racial, or sexual distinctions (v. 28)" (Guthrie, 1981, p. 656). But they have "put on Christ" (v. 27) which identifies them corporately as belonging to Christ (v. 29) which also places them in the fellowship of heirs. Thus, all believers are spiritually one in Christ.

The incorporation of believers is portrayed by various images in the New Testament. Peter describes it as a spiritual house and holy priesthood, "you yourselves like living stones are being built up as a spiritual house, to be a holy priesthood, to offer spiritual sacrifices acceptable to God through Jesus Christ" (1 Pet 2:5). And Paul calls it a building, "in whom the whole structure, being joined together, grows into a holy temple in the Lord. In him you also are being built together into a dwelling place for God by t he Spirit" (Eph 2:21–22).

"The essential point is that in spite of their various differences, all true believers are united by the Spirit to Christ and to one another. Clearly, then, the unity of genuine Christians presently exists as a spiritual reality" (Demarest, 1997, p. 342).

This explanation of the believer's incorporation into the body of Christ and the multiple descriptions of this reality suggests these practical implications related to the spiritual context of believers. First, they are one with others in the body of Christ and therefore are never alone in their quest for spiritual growth. Second, since each member of this body functions differently, there are those able to help in sanctificational growth especially in areas of weakness. Third, they can be confident that God is actively building them along with others in the body to be holy and to be a place where God dwells by his Spirit. Fourth, God has provided this environment so believers are able to grow in holiness dispelling fears having to do with lack of support.

However, the church environment, created by God for the believer's good is sometimes occupied by those who do not understand this purpose. Ford (1992) states that "the meaning of a context belief depends on the particular environmental component relevant to that achievement" (p. 130). Therefore, to have an "optimally responsive environment" certain functional elements must be in place. I apply these functional elements from Ford's writings to the church context and the following principles emerge. When believers evaluate their relational contexts, they 1) must determine if the environment aligns with their "agenda" of spiritual growth, 2) must determine if the material and informational resources needed to facilitate spiritual growth are available, and 3) must determine if the environment provides the emotional climate that supports and facilitates spiritual growth. If the context is found unresponsive and unsupportive, then motivational decisions must be made such as to grow in spite of the context, change context, or adjust one's goals.

I have suggested that Christians' beliefs regarding their union with Christ provide personal agency beliefs that affect the motivational aspect of sanctificational growth. The understanding that Christians are identified with Christ and incorporated in Christ provides the believer with the necessary realized context and capability to function in holiness or sanctification. However, this reality must not only be known, but it must also be intentionally acted upon. In the next section, an examination of Willard's VIM model will help explain the role of intentional activity in the transformational process of sanctificational growth.

A Conceptual Comparison of Romans 6:1–14 with VIM

The purpose of this comparative exercise is to see if Romans 6:1–14 fits with Dallas Willard's (2002) model of vision, intention, and means. If this fit can be determined, then perhaps Willard's model can serve as a heuristic model to better understand Paul's instruction for sanctificational growth from this passage.

Romans 6:1–14 presents the doctrine of union with Christ as an integral component to sanctificational growth. It is utilized here because its basic concept, dying and rising with Christ, "held an important place in Paul's thinking, his personal life, and his apostolic ministry" (Beasley-Murray, 1993, p. 218) so it may in our thinking as well. Additionally, it is the best known passage in which the "union with Christ" concept appears. Since Willard's model and Paul's instructions both relate to the goal of spiritual transformation, they are brought together to evaluate their fit with each other and their suitability to help explain sanctificational growth.

Willard (2002) claims that, "If we are to be spiritually formed in Christ, we must have and must implement the appropriate *vision, intention, and means*" (p. 85). This seems like a bold statement. However, if I can demonstrate that Paul's argument in Romans 6:1–14 fits the pattern of VIM, then additional support can be made for Willard's model. I may also be able to demonstrate that Paul's argument in Romans 6:1–14 provides a pattern that believers can follow leading to sanctificational growth.

The following is an overview of Willard's model of personal transformation. First, inward spiritual renovation begins with a vision of life in the kingdom of God. "The kingdom of God is the range of God's effective will, where what God wants done is done" (p. 86). This vision, then, is the "vision of life now and forever in the range of God's effective will" (p. 87). Second, "a vision of life in the kingdom through reliance upon Jesus makes it possible for us to *intend* to live in the kingdom as he did. We can actually *decide to do it*" (p. 87). This is what he means by intention. Third, "the vision and the solid intention to obey Christ will naturally lead to seeking out and applying the means to that end. Here the means in question are the means for spiritual transformation" (p. 89). This pattern not only can serve to give understanding to personal transformation but may also serve to give understanding to sanctificational growth.

To make this connection, I suggest that a) a similar concept to the idea of the vision of the kingdom of God can be extracted from Romans 6:1–6 and the doctrine of union with Christ, b) a determination of the necessity for intentionality can be made be examining the meaning of "reckoning" from Romans 6:11–13, and c) suggestions regarding the means that help fulfill the vision can be ascertained from this passage as well.

Vision

First, I suggest a conceptual relationship between Willard's vision of "life in the kingdom of God" and Paul's vision of "newness of life" (Rom 6:4). The relationship may be seen when a comparison is made between Willard's description of vision and Paul's description of living a life in Christ. Willard describes the "vision that underlies spiritual (trans)formation into Christlikeness" as

> the vision of life now and forever in the range of God's effective will—that is, *partaking* of the divine nature (2 Peter 1:4; 1 John 3:1–2) through a birth "from above" and *participating* by our actions in what God is doing now in our lifetime on earth....In everything we do we are permitted to do his work. What we are aiming for in this vision is to live fully in the kingdom of God and as fully as possible *now* and *here*, not just hereafter. (p. 87)

Living "in Christ" may relate to Willard's characteristics of vision for two reasons. First, believers are partakers with Christ in his death and burial having been "baptized into Christ Jesus" (Rom 6:4–5) at conversion. Believers are recipients of this partnership since it has been granted by God's "divine power" (2 Pet 2:1–4). Believers "partake of the divine nature" in this "baptism" that moves them "into Christ Jesus." Second, believers are participants with Christ in order to "walk in newness of life," that is, in living a new kind of life (Rom 6:4).

Though entrance into Christ is by God's divine power, one's conduct once in Christ Jesus involves effort. However, Paul includes an essential element needed to transition believers from death and burial to newness of life—the resurrection (6:4–5) in which believers participate. "Just as" Christ was raised from the dead (6:4) by the "glory" or power of God, so believers are empowered to walk in newness of life. I now look at these comparisons in more detail.

The first description of the believer's life as partaker with Christ "in the divine nature" corresponds with Paul's description of the believer's co–crucifixion and co–burial with Christ presented in Romans 6:4–5. Having been "baptized into Christ Jesus" (6:3) believers have been moved (i.e., verb with preposition *eis*) into Christ in order to become involved and participate in his actions. Baptism initiates believers into a condition in which they now become in Christ. Those who are baptized belong to Christ and are united with him (Schreiner, 1998, p. 307).

Having been moved "into Christ" believers no longer live where sin has power over them (6:2). They have died "in reference to sin" (*ta hamartia*) indicating that they have changed their state to the disadvantage or detriment of sin (Moo, 1996, p. 357). The new state of death to sin refers to being in Christ; "a decisive and final break in one's state of being" (Moo, 1996, p. 357). Being in Christ changes their relationship to sin because "Christ died to sin, once for all" (6:10), that is, he has dealt sin a fatal blow once and for all. Sin no longer moves him. Thus, because believers died to sin in Christ, they no longer have to be moved by it either. By participating in Christ's death, believers have been set free from sin's control (6:7). But this is only one portion of what transpires in their participation.

Believers in Christ were also "co–buried" with him, a reference indicating the "communality of believers rooted in a dependence upon their communality in Christ" (Dunn, 1988a, p. 313). The baptism that inaugurated believers into Christ and his death also initiated them into his burial. This is another indication of the believer's participation with Christ, this time in his burial. "Buried with him by baptism into death" could mean then that believers have been immersed into his death together with him. Burial validates that death has occurred and so are presented together (cf. 1 Cor 15:3–4).

But now there is no indication of co–resurrection though the verse states that Christ was raised from the dead. Paul seems to skip over the believer's resurrection in order to emphasize their new life. Yet, Paul states that the purpose of believer's participating in his death and burial was in order that "just as Christ was raised from the dead by the glory of the Father, we too might walk in newness of life" (6:4). There cannot be a resurrection without a death and burial. And a resurrection is necessary to live if one is dead and buried. Though believers are dead to sin by virtue of Christ's death to sin, they are also to live a new life. A resurrection must take place.

So, believers are to walk in newness of life "just as Christ was raised from the dead." New Testament scholar Thomas Schreiner (1998) states that "just as" can be considered as comparative and causal in this context. "The newness of believers' lives is grounded on the resurrection of Christ" who demonstrated new life in his resurrection. "Thus the call to live in newness of life is grounded in participating not only in Christ's death and burial but also in his resurrection" (p. 311). Again, Paul explains that believers walk in newness of life only because they are in union with Christ.

However, Paul does not actually "skip over" the believer's resurrection with Christ "for" verse 5 explains verse 4: "For if we have been united with him in a death like his, we shall certainly be united with him in a resurrection like his." "Paul's argument is that believers should walk in newness of life, not only because they participate in Christ's death and burial (vv. 2–3) but also because they shall participate in Christ's resurrection" (Schreiner, 1998, p. 312). The future tense "shall be" (*esometha*) in the phrase "we shall be united with him in the likeness of his resurrection," has stirred debate. It is difficult to see how present conduct could be affected if believers are united with Christ's resurrection only in the future. One explanation considers the death and resurrection of Christ as eschatological events that transcend time and can therefore penetrate and affect the present lives of believers (Schreiner, 1998, p. 312; Moo, 1996, p. 381–382). It is beyond the scope of this discussion to decide on the best way to resolve this issue. My single claim is that it is only in union with Christ that believers walk in newness of life whether that union is past or future. These verses support this argument.

The third description of the believer's life as participation with Christ corresponds to a new kind of living similar to participation in the kingdom also relates to the concept of walking in newness of life. By using the term "walk," Paul described this new life as a manner in which believers conduct themselves. He conveys this idea by using a word which means literally "to go here and there in walking" (i.e., "go about, walk around") or figuratively "to conduct one's life" (i.e., "comport oneself, behave, live as habit of conduct") (Danker, 2000, p. 803). In this context, the new life is demonstrated by a conduct directed by God and not directed by sin (6:12–14).

By using the phrase, "in order that" (*hina*), Paul demonstrates that the believer's conduct in newness of life is the purpose of their union with Christ's death and burial. Believers are to live a certain way as a result of dying and being buried with Christ; marked by conduct demonstrating the power of a resurrected life.

Willard describes the vision that underlies spiritual transformation into Christlikeness as living by partaking of the divine nature and participating in what God is doing now on earth. I have suggested that Paul demonstrates this vision by his explanation of the believer's union with Christ in Romans 6:1–14. Believers partake in the divine nature by their inauguration into Christ which brings about a new condition of being "in Christ." Those in Christ share in his death, burial, and resurrection so that they can conduct themselves in newness of life.

But there also seems to be a conceptual similarity between Paul's "in-Christ" concept and Willard's concept of the kingdom of God. Willard (1998) himself makes this connection.

As a disciple of Jesus I am with him, by choice and by grace, learning from him how to live in the kingdom of God. This is the crucial idea. That means, we recall, how to live within the range of God's effective will, his life flowing through mine. Another important way of putting this is to say that I am learning from Jesus to live my life as he would live my life if he were I. I am not necessarily learning to do everything he did, but I am learning how to do everything I do in the manner that he did all that he did. (p. 283)

Willard expresses both the believer's identification with Christ as a disciple and the believer's incorporation into Christ in sharing his life. The statement that God's life flows through those in the kingdom so that his will is effected is similar to Paul's statement, "It is no longer I who live, but Christ who lives in me" (Gal 2:20) and fits the analogy of the vine in John 15. But what are the similarities between this kingdom and the "in–Christ" domain?

The similarity between life in the kingdom and life in Christ may be seen as life in a new realm. I suggest that "newness of life" (Rom 6:4) made possible by the believer's union with Christ, denotes a new realm or domain that powerfully influences how believers conduct themselves similar to the kind of life they live in the kingdom of God. "'Newness of life' is a life empowered by the realities of the new age—including especially God's Spirit (Rom. 7:6)—and a life that should reflect the values of that new age" (Moo, 1996, p. 366).

Paul explains in Romans 6:13 that believers are to present themselves to God "as those who have been brought from death to life." The particle "as" denotes a comparison (Danker, 2000, p. 729) in this verse between their action of presenting themselves to God and their new life. Their action should match their position. To whom they present themselves must be consistent with a life that has been brought back from death, that is, a brought-back-from-the-dead kind of life.

However, Schreiner (1998) believes that "as" is causal, "indicating that believers should present themselves to God "because" they are alive from the dead." Though believers have not yet received the resurrection (vv. 5, 8, 12), they have already participated in the power of Christ's resurrection and thus have the ability to live a new quality of life (p. 324). Believers have been given a new kind of life with a quality, power, and purpose. This new kind of life is expounded by Demarest (1997):

As a result of the Spirit's regenerating work, the believer receives a new disposition, a new set of affections, new moral qualities, and new aspirations. The NT describes the result of this transformation as the "new self" (Eph 4:24; Col 3:10), which is the glorified Christ living his life in the believer (Gal 2:20). This new being expresses itself in an entirely new manner of life and conduct (Rom 6:24; 7:6). (p. 299)

One benefit of the believer's union with Christ is the reality that due to co–crucifixion and co–resurrection they now can live a new moral life filled with the power of the Holy Spirit, who as God's agent, raised Jesus from the dead (2 Cor 4:10–11; 5:14–21). Knowing this (Rom 6:3, 6, 9) gives believers the visionary motivation to live such a "new" life.

A new life brought about by union with Christ not only indicates that believers have become new people but also that they inhabit a new sphere. Grudem (1994) states that being "in Christ" provides dramatic changes "in the realm in which we live." He writes:

> To become a Christian is to enter the newness of the age to come, and to experience to some degree the new powers of the kingdom of God affecting every part of our lives. To be "in Christ" is to be in the new realm that Christ controls. (p. 843)

Schreiner (1998) agrees, "Indeed, by virtue of Christ's resurrection the age to come has invaded the present age, and thus even now believers should walk in newness of life" (p. 299).

The relationship between God's kingdom and living in Christ can be seen in Paul's words of Colossians 1:13, "He has delivered us from the domain of darkness and transferred us to the kingdom of his beloved Son." Richard Melick (1991), professor of New Testament and Greek, notes this relationship.

> [Paul] did not seem to distinguish between [kingdom of God and kingdom of Christ]. The kingdom of Christ is an intermediate kingdom which will someday be handed over to the Father.... [1 Cor 15:24]. The ultimate state of existence for the believer is the kingdom of God, but God planned for Christ and his kingdom to be the focus in the interval between the cross and the return of Christ.... Paul consistently spoke of the need of being in God's kingdom, and the way to do this is to be placed in the kingdom of Christ. Christ will bring the believer to God in his kingdom. (p. 207)

New Testament scholar James Dunn (1996) also notes the tension between the current kingdom of Christ which has already been accomplished and the kingdom of God which is still to be accomplished (p. 79). In other words, the kingdom of Christ is a distinct yet transitional age in which the Christian participates under the lordship of Christ. The vision of living life "in the kingdom of God" can include living "in the kingdom of Christ" made available to those in union with Christ.

From this discussion, it is possible to see the similarity between the vision of life in the kingdom of God and the vision of life in Christ. Romans 6:1–14, as a vision of living with Christ in newness of life, presents enough similarities with life in God's kingdom that the "vision" component of personal or sanctificational transformation, can be affirmed. That believers, in union with Christ, partake of Christ's life and participate in Christ's work within the realm of Christ's rule, indicates a similarity between the vision of living in God's kingdom and living in Christ.

As we move from the vision to intention, it is appropriate to mention that theologians and exegetes progress through Romans 6:1–14 in a similar manner. Though there has been critique of the use of the terminology, scholars traditionally refer to the Christian's union with Christ as "indicative" (statements of theological truth) and the commands that follow from the indicative as "imperative" (ethical commands). These are "strictly speaking grammatical labels for two of the Greek verbal mood forms" (Porter, 1993, p. 401). According to Porter (1993), professor of Religious Studies, there are two views regarding this distinction: a) the imperative proceeds from the indicative ("become what you are") or b) the believer is simultaneously in both realms (p. 401). Or the concepts can be seen as more dynamic and "inextricably interwoven" (Schreiner, 1998, p. 321).

It is outside the scope of this discussion to debate the issue any further. Yet it seems more beneficial to recognize the dynamic reality of both realms as simultaneous in sanctificational growth and in Paul's instructions in Romans 6:1–14 in part to prevent a confusing and potentially demotivating notion of "becoming what we already are."

Intention

The second stage of the transformational process, intention, is examined in light of the verbs of Romans 6:11–13. Intention has to do with the freedom to decide and with the "decision to fulfill or carry through with the intention" which brings power and order into life processes (Willard, 2002, p. 88). The believer, in union with Christ, has the capacity to decide and direct what needs to be done so sanctificational growth is given an opportunity to occur. Willard (1988) explains this capacity from his understanding of Romans 6:1–5 as a psychological condition that due to Christ's life within, the believer can "rise above" the "old person" to find motivation, organization, and direction for living. The new life in Christ enables Christians to make choices to do what is good since they have a "new force" within them freeing them from sin. Those without this new life have no choice but to be directed by sin (p. 115).

Having been set free from sin's dominion, I suggest that there is an intentional aspect to "reckoning" (Rom 6:11) whereby believers determine for themselves the extent to which their death to sin and life to God will become reality in their life. This, of course, assumes that they acknowledge or believe what is true (i.e., content), that is, that they are dead to sin and alive to God. Reckoning may have to do with the strength of this belief (i.e., the degree to which they are convinced this belief is true) and the centrality of this belief (i.e., the degree of importance this belief plays in their view of Christian living). One might say, in "reckoning," that believers are deliberately (i.e., through deliberation and reasoning) choosing (i.e., deciding and committing) to consider for themselves their death to sin and life to God in union with Christ Jesus.

The term Paul uses, *logizesthe*, is commonly translated "to consider" or "to reckon." Danker (2000) separates the original meaning of the word, *logizomai*, into three categories: 1) to determine by mathematical process: i.e., "reckon, calculate"—a commercial term meaning "credit"—or the result of calculation meaning "evaluate, estimate, look upon as, [or] consider;" 2) to give careful thought to a matter: i.e., "think (about), consider, ponder, let one's mind dwell on" with the idea of "proposing" or "purposing" in 2 Corinthians 10:2a; and 3) to hold to a view about something: i.e., "think, believe, be of the opinion" (pp. 597–598). The second meaning is adopted for the word in Romans 6:11 though the definitions "thinking about" and "considering" seem to carry the weakest meaning, unless "consider yourself dead" implies a determination for one's self. "Purposing" might be a better translation since Paul seems to exhort his readers to do more than think about being dead to sin and alive to God. It seems he is pressing them to believe this new reality with conviction through a thorough evaluation or calculation of its truth and implications for living.

Bartsch (1991) notes that *logizomai* is followed by an accusative ("your-selves") with the infinitive (implied "that" or "as") and therefore can be translated "of the opinion (= believe)" in Romans 6:11 though the sense "suppose" or "think" are not absent (p. 355). If this meaning is adopted, the formulation of deep conviction (i.e., belief) regarding the believer's death and life in Christ is imperative.

Two writers indicate that true reckoning settles at the level of the will. Dunn (1988a) sees reckoning as a firm conviction that finds expression in daily conduct. It is not a fictitious or "pretend" or "merely symbolical" event, but a settled determination to live in the light of Christ's death and in the strength of a power which has already defeated sin's reign in death (pp. 323–324). Willard (1999) understands reckoning ourselves dead to sin and alive to God as settling "in our will the question of who we intend to be" related to our identity with Christ (p. 159). These notions move reckoning from the mind or thoughts to the heart or will though neither writer bypasses the mind.

Reckoning certainly appears to involve more than just thinking correctly about Paul's instruction. This may be a necessary way to begin in this kind of deliberation. But *logizesthe* has similarities to the indirect nature of belief formation (chapter three) whereby one's beliefs result from processes of deliberation where freedom to choose what one will or will not consider is exercised. In this case however, Paul commands believers to continually determine for themselves or hold as a firm conviction that they are dead to sin and alive to God. In this process of deliberation the believer forms the resolute belief that what Paul says about the results of their union with Christ is true.

This lends strength to other terms used to describe "reckoning" such as "judge," "regard," or "calculate" in order that believers would "come to see the truth of their situation" (Morris, 1988, p. 256). Paul exhorts his readers, and all believers, to actually make the choice to appropriate Christ's death and resurrection with a "settled determination" and then to live in this reality.

Yet, this "settled determination," an act of the will, only bridges the concept of death and life in union with Christ with actual living. One cannot merely will spiritual growth or a life in Christ. It takes more than will–power. In other words, the will is involved but is not sufficient for sanctificational growth. By using a term such as "reckon," Paul portrays an effective process that most probably involves both mind and will.

Intention involves the freedom to decide and fulfill or carry through with the decision. Reckoning involves believers determining for themselves with firm conviction to live according to their identity with Christ with the implication to find ways to do so. There seems to be similarities between these two concepts both of which involve the will, the freedom to make decisions, and the power to act on those decisions.

What does it mean then to actually live in the reality of being dead to sin and alive to God? The "therefore" of verse 12 "indicates the conclusion to be drawn from the preceding argument—not a further reflection, but a practical outworking" (Dunn, 1988a, p. 336) or application of what God has done for the believer in union with Christ. Paul moves from intention to intentional action. "Paul now spells out just what it will mean for the believer to "consider" him- or herself to be "dead to sin and alive to God" (Moo, p. 381). For our purposes, we could say that Paul gives instruction regarding certain means that if followed will demonstrate death to sin and a new life in Christ.

Paul "uses two prohibitions (vv. 12 and 13a) and one command (v. 13b) to make his point" (Moo, 1996, p. 381). The first prohibition, "Let not sin therefore reign in your mortal bodies, to make you obey their passions" (v. 12), is a directive to give no rulership to sin, that is, do not let it "rule as king" (Rogers & Rogers, 1998, p. 327). Even though Christians are dead to sin by virtue of their co–crucifixion with Christ and even though sin is no longer their master and ruler, sin is still a threat to believers in their bodies and in their desires. Moreover, "Since believers have died with Christ and have his resurrection power, they are enabled to have dominion over sin even now, with the result that they do not submit to its desires" (Schreiner, 1998, p. 323).

"Members" (v. 13) has been given three meanings: 1) "body"—a synecdoche, 2) "the whole person"—parallel with "yourselves," 3) "limb"—literal translation. If "body," then the whole physical body is surrendered to God for training. If "the whole person," then not only the body but heart, mind, and natural capacities are presented to God. If "limb," then individual parts of the body, i.e., hands, feet, eyes, are presented to God. The best meaning seems to be "the whole person" since "members" parallels "yourselves" in verse 13 which would include the physical parts of the body as well.

In verse 13, Paul details how the rule of sin can be defeated in the lives of believers. "Do not present your members to sin as instruments for unrighteousness, but present yourselves to God as those who have been brought from death to life, and your members as instruments for righteousness" (v. 13). To "present" means to "place beside or put at one's disposal" (Danker, 2000, p. 778). Schreiner (1998) reaches these conclusions from this verse: 1) "Believers must consciously choose to place themselves at the disposal of their master, lord, and king," 2) "Believers should hand themselves over to God instead [of sin] and employ their members as 'weapons for the purpose of righteousness,'" and 3) "believers should present themselves to God 'because' they are alive from the dead" (p. 324). Consistently and continually presenting one's whole self to God, keeps sin from reigning over the believer's life.

Intention involves the freedom to decide and carry through with the intention. The believer, in union with Christ, has the capacity to decide and direct what needs to be done so sanctificational growth is given an opportunity to occur. The new life in Christ enables Christians to make choices to do what is good since they have a "new force" within them freeing them from sin.

Having been set free from sin's dominion, I have suggested that there is an intentional aspect to "reckoning" whereby believers determine for themselves the extent to which their death to sin and life to God will become reality in their life. For Christians "reckoning" includes deliberately (i.e., through deliberation and reasoning) choosing (i.e., deciding and committing) to consider for themselves their death to sin and life to God in union with Christ Jesus.

Paul proceeds to describe what it will mean for believers to "consider" themselves "dead to sin and alive to God." In the concluding verses, Paul gives directives that when practiced will prevent sin from mastering the believer's life and will allow one to be used for righteousness while demonstrating the power of a resurrected life.

Paul's imperatives fit well with the intention phase of Willard's VIM. Reckoning, resisting sin, and presenting oneself to God are choices believers are asked to make and commitments that need to be made with the intention to carry them out.

Means

The next stage of Willard's model focuses on means. In the case we are addressing, the imperatives of verses 11–13 not only indicate decisions and intentions that need to be obeyed, but seem also to indicate some of the means necessary for "walking in newness of life" or living righteously in sanctificational growth. "Reckoning" and "resisting sin" could be considered essential ways to prevent sin from having dominion over believer's lives (Rom 6:14). However, a critical means seems to be the last imperative from Paul which includes believers choosing to present to God their members as instruments for righteousness (Rom 6:13).

There are two primary ways to understand Paul's statement. 1) The place where sin reigns is in "your mortal body" (v. 12), (i.e., the physical body), therefore, "the members" of verse 13 refers to one's physical limbs. 2) "Body" means the whole person since "members" and "yourselves" (v. 13) are apparently synonymous and since the "desires" (v. 12) are not limited to bodily ones alone (Schreiner, 1998, p. 323). In this case, a regular presentation of one's self to God seems to prevent the domination of sin and allows one to become an instrument (tool or weapon) for righteousness.

However, Willard (1988) adopts the first meaning as referring to "our body and its parts" that need to be presented to God as instruments of righteousness.

> As those who have been through the experience of putting the "old person" to death and have found new life as a reliable fact beyond it, we are able to submit our body and its parts to God as instruments of righteousness…we consciously direct our bodies in a manner that will ensure that it eventually will come "automatically" to serve righteousness as it previously served sin automatically.
>
> Here . . . we are facing something that will not be done for us, though in our effort we'll find gracious strength beyond ourselves. (pp. 117–118)

The key to this kind of "automatic" righteous living is "practice"—"not only putting our body through the motions of actions *directly* commanded by our Lord" but also "engaging in whatever other activities may prepare us to carry out his commands" (p. 119). He continues:

this is where the standard, well-recognized spiritual disciplines become involved. These disciplines constitute the *indirect*, yet vitally necessary submission of our body and its members to righteousness. . . . But such efforts, while disciplinary in effect, are more expressions *of* spiritual life than they are disciplines *for* it. Discipline, strictly speaking, is activity carried on to prepare us indirectly for some activity other than itself. We do not practice the piano to practice the piano well, but to play it well. (pp. 119–120)

In chapter three, the indirect nature of belief and character formation was discussed. One can now see how the core of our spiritual life can be influenced through the indirect means of spiritual disciplines. Paul's command to "let not sin therefore reign in your mortal bodies, to make you obey their passions" or desires (Rom 6:12) can be fulfilled as believers practice verse 13 by presenting their whole selves and each bodily member (e.g., eyes, hands, feet, ears) to God through spiritual disciplines such as fasting, solitude, prayer, or simplicity. Regular engagement in these practices makes obeying one's desires less and less likely—gradually changing one's character.

Other means can be offered by adapting Willard's (2002, pp. 90–91) writings on the matter of means as applied to "walking in newness of life."

1. Not all means are directly under the believer's control since some are the actions of God toward believers and in believers.
2. Believers can retrain their thinking by study and meditation on Christ himself especially his life, teaching, death, burial, and resurrection.
3. Believers can learn about and meditate upon the lives of well-known "saints" who have learned to live according to Romans 6:1–14.
4. Believers can pay attention to Christians who do not practice the principles of VIM and Romans 6:1–14 and learn from their mistakes.
5. Believers can pray that God will directly work in their inner being to change the things that will enable them to walk in newness of life.

By engaging these "bodily" means in dependence on the Spirit of God while recognizing their union with Christ affords the opportunity for believers to walk a new life because they intend to. Though Paul's instructions regarding sanctification in Romans 6:1–14 do not fit exactly Willard's VIM model, there is at least a conceptual relationship that can be seen and a general pattern that can be followed.

Other Biblical Passages

This general pattern of personal transformation may be observed in other Pauline literature. The purpose of this section is to introduce potential biblical support for the VIM model from passages other than Romans 6. Therefore, the following passages only introduce the possibility of relationship and cannot be fully examined.

In 2 Corinthians 3:7–18, Paul explains the glory and freedom of the new covenant available to the one who "turns to the Lord" (v. 16) in contrast to the less glorious and veiled ministry of the old covenant. The passage ends with a statement of transformation that can take place to all who have "turned to the

Lord" and are free in the Spirit (v. 17). "And we all, with unveiled face, behold-ing the glory of the Lord, are being transformed into the same image from one degree of glory to another. For this comes from the Lord who is the Spirit" (v. 18). Here, the vision is the glorified God or the glory of Christ who reflects God's glory; a vision that translates into a life lived to the glory of God. Barnett (1997) describes the vision:

> The One "we all" see mirrored from God, though different from us, yet corre-sponds with us who see him. It is a vision of who we shall be (cf. 1 John 3:2). Through the gospel the one whom we see as in a mirror is the glorified human, the Lord Jesus Christ, who is the glorified, reflected image of God. As "we be-hold [him] as in a mirror," we are transformed into "the same image." (p. 206)

Yet, this transformation is not an automatic process. It is the believers' re-sponsibility to "see" Jesus Christ, the image of God and to understand their part in the process of transformation. This seems to correspond with the intention and means aspect of Willard's VIM pattern of spiritual transformation. Again, Barnett states:

> Paul makes it clear that we must understand our transformation to be the will of God for us and that we should actively cooperate with him in bringing to reality the eternal destiny for which we were predestined (Rom 12:1–2, 28–30). Our transformation is nothing else than a transformation into the moral and spiritual likeness of the now glorified Christ. (p. 208)

Paul also stresses that this process of transformation is only possible in the Holy Spirit and by his work (vv. 17–18). Transformation into the image of Christ is again shown to be a synergistic process.

In Galatians 5:16–25, Paul presents the vision of living by the Spirit (v. 25). He contrasts this kind of life to walking according to the desires of the flesh (vv. 16–23). However, a life in the Spirit demonstrates itself by conduct governed by the Spirit (v. 25). Intentionality is an element of this conduct as believers decide to live this way. Bruce (1982) explains:

> Walking by the Spirit is the outward manifestation, in action and speech, of living by the Spirit. Living by the Spirit is the root; walking by the Spirit is the fruit, and that fruit is nothing less than the practical reproduction of the character (and therefore the conduct) of Christ in the lives of his people. (p. 257)

> It is because they are Christ's in the sense of being members of Christ, incorporated [en Christo], that they have 'crucified the flesh'. The aorist probably indicates their participation in Christ's historical crucifixion. (p. 256)

Additionally, the crucifixion of the flesh also has a practical element im-plicit in this passage. As Paul states in Romans 6:11, "reckon yourselves dead to sin but alive to God in Christ Jesus," and Colossians 3:5, "put to death therefore your members that are on earth." "What has been effected once for all by the cross of Christ must be worked out in practice" (Bruce, 1982, p. 256).

Intentionality is suggested in verse 25 ("If we live by the Spirit, let us also walk by the Spirit") where the Spirit is said to be the source of our life and therefore is to direct our life as we live it.

A vision of living in Christ is portrayed in Ephesians 4:17–32. Together, intentional actions and means such as putting off one's old self (v. 22), being renewed in the spirit of one's mind (v. 23), and putting on the new man (v. 24), result in Christlike qualities and conduct (vv. 25–32).

The personal testimony of Paul in Philippians 3:10–4:1 suggests his personal vision for living—to know Christ—which controls his conduct. If believers accept his invitation to follow his example (v. 17), they, too, will seek to live in Christ seeking to understand him and experience him by the Spirit. Intentionality and means are seen in the imperatives to "think this way" (v. 15) and "stand firm...in the Lord" (4:1).

The vision of living a new life in Christ ("your life is hidden with Christ in God" and "Christ who is your life") is presented in Colossians 3:1–17. Intention and means are seen by the instructions to "seek the things that are above, where Christ is" (v. 1) and "set you minds on things that are above" (v. 2) resulting in Christlike qualities and holy conduct (vv. 5–17).

These scriptural passages introduce the idea that the VIM pattern may be supported by other Pauline writings related to spiritual maturity. Further analysis of these passages is needed to determine the viability of this notion.

Not only does the VIM model find viability in Scripture, but it also seems to fit the notion of the indirect nature of belief formation. One cannot become what one envisions by direct means, that is, by thinking or trying to fit into the vision one has about one's self or environment. We cannot form our beliefs simply by willing to do so. However, the VIM model suggests that by indirect "means" intentionally engaged, the vision may be realized. Additionally, it seems that this is the only way to find success in the pursuit of a vision. Intentionally practicing appropriate means related to the vision one has of the life God desires will make the fulfillment of the vision possible.

Properly understood, a "mean" need not become a legalistic practice. Legalism "commonly denotes preoccupation with form at the expense of substance" which is often demonstrated by a reliance upon human endeavor at the expense of God's work of grace (Deasley, 1996, p. 478). Legalism may also indicate that a believer is slavishly following a set of methods in order to earn merit with God (Erickson, 1985, p. 978). One who legalistically practices certain means also may use these means to measure the sanctificational condition of other believers.

In response to the misuse of means, I suggest that God's design for sanctification always includes his grace working through means in a synergistic process. Therefore, means are not ends in themselves but training practices or disciplined paths to the vision's end. The believer's concern is not to become an expert in a particular practice but to become more of what is envisioned. Nor are means a way of earning merit with God but are a way of putting forth the effort that is needed if sanctificational growth is to be experienced knowing that human effort is involved and that believers are already secure "in Christ" (i.e., no human merit is possible or required). Nor are means to be used as rigid standards by which to measure others' conduct. Using means in this way makes too much of them by placing them in a position from which judgments are made. This is not the purpose of means. Means, such as spiritual disciplines, are usually applied to areas of weakness in one's character. This suggests that their purpose relates to the humble recognition of one's flaws while in legalism their purpose seems to relate to a prideful view of one's self.

Summary

The study in this chapter suggests that believers are capable of living a life of righteousness out of the resources God provides in union with Christ. This chapter presented an examination of the "union with Christ" motif integrated with two models of personal change. First, integrating Ford's personal agency beliefs with the "union with Christ" concept suggests that there is a fit between these concepts providing support for the notion that union with Christ entails the concepts of capability and context as described in Ford's theory. Second, integrating the union with Christ concept as presented in Romans 6:1–14 with Willard's VIM suggests a fit between these concepts. Willard's VIM seems to provide a heuristic model for Paul's instruction for sanctificational growth in this passage.

This integrative exercise also suggests that the direct interaction of these concepts mutually reinforce one another. This results in a more comprehensive understanding of sanctification and in particular, progressive sanctification. It is essential that believers live with a settled determination that in union with Christ they are capable of sanctificational growth as they view their capabilities and environment as supportive to this goal and as they live in Christ employing effective means for spiritual growth.

CHAPTER 6

EDUCATION AND MINISTRY IMPLICATIONS OF HUMAN PARTICIPATION AND UNION WITH CHRIST

This book has been written within the field of Christian education. Because scholars within this field constantly deal with the issues of theory and practice, it is appropriate that this final chapter provide an introduction to some practices reflecting the concepts examined in previous chapters. However, to demonstrate that the practices themselves are grounded in reliable theory, I have engaged in dialogue with some experts regarding certain relevant and practical notions related to Christian education, spiritual disciplines, and church ministry that apply. Interspersed throughout the discussion are "flash backs" to ideas already examined that find application here.

Most notably, Willard's VIM model provides the structure for discussing the ministry practices highlighted in this chapter such as worship and small groups. This model furnishes the lens through which these ministries are examined. Throughout this study I have suggested that the VIM model fits with the theological and biblical concepts of progressive sanctification. I now suggest that it may also support the direction of educational or church ministries with the goal of personal transformation of those involved. Though the principles of VIM may have profound implications for many church ministries such as missions, youth ministries, leadership development, discipleship, Sunday School (curriculum, training, teaching) and other activities such as budgeting or planning, I will focus on the broad ministry categories of worship and small groups.

The concept of sanctificational growth fits with a commonly stated priority of Christian education. Christian educator Roy Zuck (1998) writes that

> many of Paul's goal–oriented statements and exhortations show his deep concern not only about what his readers knew, but also about what they were to be and to do. These aims may be summarized in one phrase: to foster spiritual growth and maturity. This is essentially the same goal Jesus had in his ministry. . . . [Christlikeness] is the goal every teacher should have for each of his or her students: that each student become like Christ by coming "to know him better" (Eph. 1:17) . . . lack of spiritual development should be of concern to teachers. (p. 114–115)

According to Christian educator Nevin Harner (1939), "Christian education is a reverent attempt to discover the divinely ordained process by which individuals grow in Christlikeness, and to work with that process" (p. 20). The examination of human participation in progressive sanctification has sought to address this particular goal of Christian education. The first five chapters have been a quest to discover aspects of God's design for sanctificational growth in which believers participate. This chapter examines some practical means by which Christian educators, practitioners, and believers work with this "divinely ordained process."

Review of Preceding Chapters

Human participation in sanctificational growth can be seen in the following brief summary of the chapters in this study. Each chapter makes one major claim and in this review each one includes an application or example drawn from concepts presented in Romans 6:1–14.

In chapter two the claim was made that believers participate at some level in sanctificational synergism. God and believers work in a "cooperative" manner (with God supervising) towards the pursuit of Christlikeness. For example, God has provided incorporation of the believer into Christ as a result of Christ's death, burial, and resurrection. Yet, reckoning is something Christians do along with obeying the other imperatives presented throughout Scripture.

Chapter three argued that believers are able to participate in the sanctificational process due to possessing free will. Decisions, however, are made in relationship to one's character. Believers possess the capability by virtue of their free will to decide or intend to grow spiritually by developing beliefs and character that reflect Jesus Christ. In reckoning themselves dead to sin and alive to God in union with Christ, believers are able to determine, by the power of the Holy Spirit, what they will be.

In chapter four I claim that believers participate by utilizing their personal agency beliefs which contribute to motivation for sanctificational growth. Christians can see themselves in union with Christ as having the capability and the personal and corporate context for sanctificational growth.

Finally, in chapter five the integrative nature of this study is demonstrated in two ways. First, by explaining the union with Christ concept and examining its fit with personal agency beliefs suggesting that believers are motivated toward sanctificational growth by viewing themselves in union with Christ. Second, the key passage for instruction regarding union with Christ, Romans 6:1–14, is examined to determine its fit with Willard's VIM model. The study suggests that Paul's instructions in this passage teach a way of spiritual transformation compatible with the concepts of vision, intention, and means presented by Willard. These models contain concepts such as synergism, belief and character formation, free will, and intentionality that were examined in other chapters. These models and concepts fit well enough together to illustrate their mutual support and their ability to fill in the details such that a more comprehensive understanding of sanctificational growth results.

Sanctification and Educational Implications

There seems to be a relationship between sanctificational growth and the educational process. A few aspects of this relationship are explored in this section. The practical nature of Christian education will be introduced as implications of this study for education are explored.

One characteristic of Christian education is its concern that theory be put into practice. Christian educators seem to know intuitively and experientially that good practice derives from good theory and that only the activation of both results in life change. Applied to this study, then, having set forth the theory that believers participate in progressive sanctification through making choices, developing character and belief, and acknowledging with settled determination their own capability and environment to live in Christ, it is now necessary to present practical means whereby this participation takes place.

In the introduction to this chapter, two Christian educators (Zuck and Harner) were quoted indicating that a primary goal of Christian education is Christian maturity or Christlikeness. The purpose of Christian education is not only to instruct students or disciples, but also to see their lives transformed. As this study suggests, it is in the training of one's actions that one's character (i.e., set of beliefs and desires) is affected. Therefore, for one's inner life to be changed one must intentionally engage in actions that effectively address issues of heart (i.e., will and spirit) and mind (i.e., thoughts and emotions). Therefore, what practical acts can one engage in that will affect heart and mind so that one becomes more like Christ? Before this question is addressed, there needs to be a reminder that this change process is a synergistic operation as believers work with God's work of life transformation.

Synergism and the Educational Process

Having examined the synergistic nature of sanctificational growth in chapter two, we are reminded that maturity for the believer takes place as God's efforts supervise and guide human cooperation. The educational process in Christian education acknowledges and operates within the same synergistic framework. There are educational implications to human participation and synergism for sanctificational growth. These implications relate to the learning process, the teacher, the learner, and learning outcomes. Each of these elements of the educational process, as far as Christians understand education, involves both divine and human roles.

The human role involves a cognitive level of learning which includes the need to acquire new information and to develop the intellectual skills that enable students to process facts. At this level, three degrees of learning are recognized: awareness, understanding, and wisdom (Issler and Habermas, 1994, pp. 31–37). Christian educators understand that the last two degrees involve experiencing the information or process so that a truth is lived experientially as well as known intellectually. Thus, the behavioral level of learning is introduced. Learning relates to bodily actions and includes learned competencies. "Learning good habits and persevering in the routines of our lifestyle contribute to the development of Christian character," according to Christian educators Issler and Habermas (pp. 37–38).

Two additional levels of learning, the affective (i.e., emotions and attitudes) and dispositional (i.e., values and tendencies to act), involve the intentional actions of character development in which the emotions, intellect, and will are trained until habits or excellences for Christlikeness are formed. The learner is responsible to seek means that help bring this process to reality.

However, the Christian's learning activities are to be engaged by faith in the work of God in the process. One of the distinctives of Christian education is the acknowledgement of the role of the Holy Spirit in the educational process. Christian education professor Dennis Williams (2001) presents some similarities between secular and Christian education such as the same learning theories, methodologies, approaches to learning, and the desire for learning or change. But he also points out one major difference:

> There is a difference, however, because of the role of the Holy Spirit in Christian education. Through the illumination of the Holy Spirit, believers are shown the truth of God's Word, and this is not present in secular education. Both secular and Christian educators may use similar methodologies, but this does not make them the same. Christian education is indeed unique because of the ministry of the Holy Spirit. (p. 132–133)

Biblical expositor Roy Zuck (1998) elaborates that the three indispensable factors that make Christian education dynamic and distinctive are a) God's written revelation, b) regeneration, and c) the ministry of the Holy Spirit (p. 2). Yet, he considers the Holy Spirit as the indispensable agent for effective teaching and Christian living.

> The Holy Spirit, working through the Word of God, is the spiritual dynamic for Christian living. If the Holy Spirit is not at work through the teacher and through the written Word of God, then our teaching remains virtually ineffective and is little different from secular teaching. (p. 6)

As in progressive sanctification, the learning process for Christians is complex due to both human and divine involvement in the process. Issler and Habermas (1994) provide a basic definition of learning that includes both agents of learning along with some of the components that have been addressed in this study.

> Learning for Christians is change that is facilitated through deliberate or incidental experience, under the supervision of the Holy Spirit, in which they acquire and regularly integrate developmentally appropriate knowledge, attitudes, values, emotions, skills, habits, and dispositions into an increasingly Christ-like life. (p. 23)

The purpose of this reminder is to affirm the reality of synergism not only for sanctificational growth but for all areas of Christian learning. For example, an understanding of synergism influences the roles of the human teacher and the student in the educational process. Issler and Habermas (1994) discuss the roles of the Divine Teacher, the human teacher, and the learner.

> Identifying exactly how the Divine Teacher works alongside the human teacher and within the student is difficult to unravel. . . . In some cases, God directly (i.e., immediately) intervenes to accomplish his purposes. . . . But in most cases, God works through the natural laws within his creation, and particularly through human beings (i.e., mediately) . . . The norm for us as human teachers, then, is to teach to the best of our abilities, as God enables both teacher and student. (p. 19)

The interplay of divine and human effort in the educational process also influences learning outcomes. For both sanctificational and Christian educational change the desired outcome is similar—having to do with God's will or the character of Christ. Christian education professor Robert Pazmiño (1997) defines Christian education including the elements of synergism and divine outcomes.

> Christian education is the deliberate, systematic, and sustained divine and human effort to share or appropriate the knowledge, values, attitudes, skills, sensitivities, and behaviors that comprise or are consistent with the Christian faith. It fosters the change, renewal, and reformation of persons, groups, and structures by the power of the Holy Spirit to conform to the revealed will of God as expressed in the Scriptures and preeminently in the person of Jesus Christ, as well as any outcomes of that effort. (p. 87)

If Pazmiño's analysis of the educational process is valid, the purpose of Christian educators is to help others follow the will of God and become more like Jesus Christ by the power of the Holy Spirit. The outcome of Christian educational efforts fits with the purposes of sanctificational growth.

How then can a teacher and student practically acknowledge and develop competencies related to this synergistic component? Perhaps the key is prayer. Prayer before and, when appropriate, during and after learning sessions is an opportunity for the teacher and student to intentionally bring to mind notions of God which bear upon the present educational setting. This is an opportunity to acknowledge God's presence and enablement in the learning process while intentionally training the will (e.g., choosing to focus on God), intellect (e.g., recalling aspects of God's omnipotence), and emotions (e.g., expressing love for God) of teacher and student. In prayer, both teacher and student are able to submit to the Holy Spirit for his empowerment to teach or learn.

Not only would it be appropriate to practice this kind of prayer in class but also outside the classroom as teachers develop their semester syllabus and daily lesson plans. It would be wise to pray like this before and during the process. Students can also recognize synergism in prayer as they read, study their notes, prepare for tests, or fulfill assignments. The whole educational process would benefit from recognizing divine-human synergism.

Competencies could also be developed through well–developed devotionals presented at the beginning of the learning session. This exercise demonstrates the teacher's awareness of God "at work" in the context of the learning process. An awareness of the Spirit's direction and a submission to the Spirit could be genuinely vocalized and practiced in these devotionals. Such practices also provide an opportunity for teachers and students to present themselves to God daily (or more often) when engaged in the educational process. Acknowledging God as the creator of human beings and their minds, hearts, wills, and bodies may demonstrate a humble acceptance of his role in the educational process. This acknowledgement also allows for the recognition of human weaknesses which reinforces the need for God's involvement. If it is true that any kind of Christian growth takes place due to divine–human synergistic activity, then teachers and students need to recognize that reality regularly.

Belief Formation and Educational Implications

One task of Christian teachers is to help students fully develop a Christian worldview (Issler and Habermas, 1994, p. 26). As was examined in chapter three, a worldview is formed by assumptions and beliefs that reflect an individual's view of reality. This view of reality is constantly being adjusted. One principle of belief formation is that beliefs are normally changed by indirect means. Swinburne (1997) writes, "It is true that while I cannot change my beliefs at an instant, I can set about trying to change them over a period and I may have some success in this" (p. 127). Belief formation "over a period" seems to relate to an educational process that includes the consideration of new information.

So, learners need to intentionally engage in this "indirect" process to change beliefs and bring a closer view of reality into their worldview. They can follow Swinburne's (1997) notion that beliefs can be changed indirectly by:

1. Looking for more evidence knowing that might lead to a change in their beliefs
2. Deliberately seeking to cultivate a belief, for example, by looking selectively for favorable evidence, and then trying to forget the selective character of the investigation
3. Trying to adopt new standards for assessing old evidence.

Exposing oneself to new evidence characterizes what is to take place in the learning process. When a student begins a course of study he or she is choosing to look for new information in various educational experiences (e.g., listening to lecture, reading literature, engaging in classroom discussions and group projects, or making presentations). The teacher uses these methods to enhance the learning experience and the learner engages them in order to form or change beliefs. And as Moreland (1997) writes, "if these kinds of changes in belief are what cause a change in my character and behavior, then I will be transformed by these changes" (p. 75).

Issler and Habermas (1994) claim that the most popular view of learning includes the acquisition of new information (p. 31). But learning also involves developing new thinking skills and, for the Christian, applying this knowledge to life. Thus, cognitive mastery includes, "(1) awareness (being conscious of some concept); (2) understanding (having a better perception of a concept's meaning and significance; and (3) wisdom (consistently using this information to make an important decision" (p. 31). New information (i.e., information outside our current worldview), when processed in this manner, may help create new worldview beliefs, confirm current beliefs, or eliminate wrong beliefs. However, the student must first be willing to consider the new concept.

The same may hold true for the process of sanctificational growth. Biblical and theological evidence that is presently unknown to believers must be considered for beliefs to be formulated or changed and for sanctificational growth to take place. Whether in the university classroom through discussion or lecture or in a congregational setting through Bible studies or sermons, the instructor and the learner can engage in the process of belief formation by opening their minds to new information. Combined with the Holy Spirit's work of illumination and enablement, their character and behavior can be positively affected as they grow in Christlikeness.

However, learning by examining new evidence, cultivating new beliefs, and establishing new standards of assessment takes place only through intentional effort. Sanctificational growth can only occur when believers learn. Therefore, believers need to be students of Jesus Christ and the Scriptures by any means available—Bible studies, on–line courses, formal college or seminary training, seminars, adult education classes, books, sermons, or conferences. In the process of learning, guided by the Holy Spirit, believers' lives are changed.

Public Worship and Sanctificational Growth

With the understanding that believers are capable of participating in God's work of producing spiritual growth and that their participation is essential to this growth, this section examines the concept of worship for the fostering of spiritual dispositions leading to spiritual growth. The activities related to the Lord's Supper are practical means by which believers intentionally participate so that spiritual growth results, though indirectly. This activity is also an example of the synergistic nature of sanctificational growth. The following discussion will be framed by concepts already discussed related to Willard's VIM model.

Vision Related to Living in God's Presence

For spiritual transformation to take place, a vision of perpetually being in God's presence in public worship and daily activities seems to fit a life in God's kingdom and life as the church. Paul gives instructions to the church regarding worship.

Let the word of Christ dwell in you richly, teaching and admonishing one another in all wisdom, singing psalms and hymns and spiritual songs, with thankfulness in your hearts to God. And whatever you do, in word or deed, do everything in the name of the Lord Jesus, giving thanks to God the Father through him. (Col 3:16–17)

The vision of this kind of life will be followed by an intention to live this way and an incorporation of appropriate means to do it. This will usually involve the regular attendance and genuine participation in a worship service in which living in God's presence is emphasized. Not only can VIM provide a model for personal transformation, it can also be a structure upon which ministries, such as the worship service, can be formed.

The need for believers to fully participate in worship may be observed in the typical evangelical worship service on any given Sunday. Passivity and apathy may characterize many who gather for the church meeting. Since the primary purpose of worship is to acknowledge and glorify God, passivity is an inappropriate disposition for true worship. Four Greek terms provide an understanding of worship in Scripture.

1. *Latreuō* refers to activities of service; "of the carrying out of religious duties . . . by human beings" (Danker, 2002, p. 587) towards God (Matt 4:10; Luke 1:74, 4:8; Acts 7:7, 24:14, 27:23; Heb 7:14; Rev 7:15, 22:3).

2. *Proskuneō* means "to express in attitude or gesture one's complete dependence on or submission to a high authority figure, *(fall down and) worship, do obeisance to, prostrate oneself before, do reverence to, welcome respectfully*" (Danker, 2002, p. 882) (Matt 4:9; Luke 4:7; Rev 9:20, 13:4, 8, 12; 20:4).

3. *Sebō* means to "express in gestures, rites, or ceremonies one's allegiance or devotion to deity" (Danker, 2002, p. 917) (Matt 15:9; Mark 7:7; Acts 18:13; 19:27).

4. *Eusebeō* refers to showing "uncommon reverence or respect, *show profound respect for someone*" (Danker, 2002, p. 413).

Each of these terms is used in reference to God indicating the various human expressions of God's worthiness. Worship is therefore "seen as the direct acknowledgement or realization of who God is and how he deals with humankind" (Anthony, 2001, p. 731).

Scripture indicates that the primary focus of worship is God. A sampling of verses indicates the God-centered nature of true worship:

Ascribe to the Lord, O clans of the peoples, ascribe to the Lord glory and strength! Ascribe to the Lord the glory due his name; bring an offering and come before him! Worship the Lord in the splendor of holiness; tremble before him, all the earth. (1 Chron 16:27–30a, cf. Ps 96:7–9)

Oh come, let us worship and bow down; let us kneel before the Lord, our Maker! (Ps 95:6)

Therefore let us be grateful for receiving a kingdom that cannot be shaken, and thus let us offer to God acceptable worship, with reverence and awe, for our God is a consuming fire. (Heb 12:28–29)

I, John, am the one who heard and saw these things. And when I heard and saw them, I fell down to worship at the feet of the angel who showed them to me, but he said to me, "You must not do that! I am a fellow servant with you and your brothers the prophets, and with those who keep the words of this book. Worship God. (Rev 22:8–9)

True worship, then, is to be understood as entailing a vision of God that reflects and responds to his revealed character and work. It is a vision of a life centered and focused on God with thoughts and ideas of him that correspond with his true being and with decisions, actions, and relationships that acknowledge him. This seems to be the kind of life that believers entered through faith in Jesus Christ that Scripture often calls "eternal life."

Jesus clarifies the meaning of "eternal life" by stating that it includes knowing "the only true God and Jesus Christ" who was sent by God (John 17:3). This is the way believers are to live now and eternally. New Testament scholar D. A. Carson (1991) elaborates:

> Eternal life turns on nothing more and nothing less than knowledge of the true God. Eternal life is not so much everlasting life as personal knowledge of the Everlasting One. . . . To know God is to be transformed, and thus to be introduced to a life that could not otherwise be experienced. . . . Nor is this knowledge of God and of Jesus Christ merely intellectual, mere information (though it invariably includes information). . . . it is clear that the knowledge of God and of Jesus Christ entails fellowship, trust, personal relationship, faith. (p. 556)

Thus the vision of living distinguished by a growing knowledge of God seems to include a life of worship which centers its attention upon God. As believers engage in a life of worshipping the Lord they experience aspects of God essential to life. David describes his own experience of continual worship and the telling personal effects.

> I will bless the Lord at all times; his praise shall continually be in my mouth. My soul makes its boast in the Lord; let the humble hear and be glad. Oh, magnify the Lord with me, and let us exalt his name together! I sought the Lord and he answered me and delivered me from all my fears. Those who look to him are radiant, and their faces shall never be ashamed. This poor man cried, and the Lord heard him and saved him out of all his troubles. . . . Oh, taste and see that the Lord is good! Blessed is the man who takes refuge in him! Oh, fear the Lord, you his saints, for those who fear him have not lack! (Ps 34:1–6, 8–9)

Intentionality and Means Related to Worship

Additionally, the genuine worship of God seems to include the intentional efforts of believers who engage in means resulting in sanctificational growth.

Paul indicates the sanctificational aspect of worship when he appeals to the believers in Rome "to present your bodies a living sacrifice holy and acceptable to God, which is your spiritual worship" (Rom 12:1). From Romans 6:13, presenting one's whole self, including bodily "members," was seen as an intentional means to becoming an instrument of righteousness. Here, presenting one's body to God is seen also as an act of worship. Worship includes a presentation of one's whole being to God which itself is a work of progressive sanctification or spiritual transformation.

The emphasis of sanctificational growth in worship may be a missing component of the worship experience. The need for full, "whole–person" participation by those gathered for worship may be met by both an emphasis on intentionality and on spiritual growth in public worship. In other words, not only is there a need for the participants to be intentional in genuine worship, the leaders who guide the worship experience also need to be intentional in their use of appropriate means so that God's presence is acknowledged and so that God's work of transformation may take place.

A general observation regarding the relationship of worship and spiritual growth is noted by Christian educator Kenneth Gangel (1994) who acknowledges the lack of proper participation in worship.

> [We need to] recognize the paucity of participation not only in order of service, but through intentional spiritual formation in public worship. In the practice of spiritual formation we bring something to God, even if it be only our wretched sinful selves in desperate need of forgiveness. We also bring praise and adoration in whereas the former tends to be a private discipline, the latter binds us together in participation.
>
> Perhaps corporate worship will take a nudge toward progress if Christians begin to realize that worship does not consist merely of Bible study or any other single activity. Certainly *prayer* will be involved, as will *praise*, but a third word beginning with that same letter clamors for more attention— *participation*. (pp. 115–116)

Worship is essentially, but not exclusively, a human activity involving human effort. The basic meaning of worship refers to "the action of human beings in expressing homage to God because he is worthy of it," according to New Testament exegete I. H. Marshall (1996b, p. 1250). It includes such activities as "adoration, thanksgiving, prayers of all kinds, the offering of sacrifice and the making of vows" (Marshall, 1996b, p. 1250). "The essence of worship is the intentional ascription of worth, service, and reverence to the Lord," writes Moreland (1997, p. 157).

Two aspects of worship are acknowledged in these descriptions. First, it is an activity of intention as believers decide to worship and then do what they intend. It is a choice or decision to honor the Lord. However, as with all means of spiritual growth, worship entails interaction with all aspects of the human personality—will, spirit, mind, thought, emotion, and body—directed to God.

Second, worship involves a work of God in which he initiates and supervises the activity by revealing himself and by energizing it through the Holy Spirit. Because God "is the greatest being that could possible exist" (Moreland,

1997, p. 158), worship is not only what human beings do or give to God but is to be carried out in response to God's person and activity. "Worship is a human response to a gracious God, and it needs to be placed in this context if it is to be properly understood" (Marshall, 1996b, p. 1250). Marshall continues:

> Nowadays, however, 'worship' is used to describe any kind of interaction between God and his people, expressed in (but not confined to) cultic or formal activity by a religious group or individuals. It therefore includes not only a human approach to God but also the communications of God with his people. (p. 1250)

For worship to result in sanctificational growth there must be evidence of effort and response to God in a synergistic process whereby God supervises and empowers the worshippers and their activity. This includes not only the activity of public, corporate worship, but any activity whether eating a meal (1 Cor 10:31) or working (Col 3:23–24). Moreland (1997) even relates the development of our human faculties to worship. *"God is worthy of the very best efforts we can give Him in offering our respect and service through the cultivation of our total personality, including our minds"* (p. 159). Our primary concern here, however, is corporate worship.

In dialogue with the Samaritan woman (John 4:1–30), Jesus speaks of the need for "true" worshipers of the Father to worship him "in spirit and truth" (vv. 24–25) since the Father is seeking such people (v. 23) and since God is spirit (v. 24). "Genuine worship is spiritual," writes New Testament scholar Leon Morris (1995, p. 236). But, what does this mean?

Morris argues:

> It is not likely that "spirit" here means the Holy Spirit (though the Spirit does help our worship, Rom. 8:26ff.). It is the human spirit that is in mind. One must worship, not simply outwardly by being in the right place and taking up the right attitude, but in one's spirit. (p. 239)

If Willard's (2002) view of the human "spirit," which includes the dimensions of will and heart, is accepted, then understanding Jesus' words becomes clearer. He claims that the will or heart (spirit) that is being transformed into Christlikeness is characterized by a

> *single–minded and joyous devotion to God and his will, to what God wants for us—and to service to him and to others because of him—is what the will transformed into Christlikeness looks like.* That is the outcome of Christian spiritual formation with reference to the will, heart, or spirit. And his outcome becomes our *character* when it has become the governing response of every dimension of our being. Then we can truly be said to have "put on Christ." (p. 143)

True worship incorporates these aspects of Christlike transformation noted by Willard—a single-minded and joyous devotion to Christ (2 Cor 11:3), service (worship) in line with God's will (Rom 12:2), and a "governing response" of praise, thankfulness, or glorifying God that becomes our character (1 Cor

10:31). Thus, worship is not simply done in a particular time, place, or mood, but becomes a way of living from an inner spirit (heart, will) that is being renewed day by day (2 Cor 4:15–16).

Paul provides instruction regarding the interaction of mind and spirit in genuine praise and worship. "I will pray with my spirit, but I will pray with my mind also; I will sing praise with my spirit, but I will sing with my mind also" (1 Cor 14:15). His example demonstrates that all dimensions of the human being need to be involved if true worship is to occur. The believer's thoughts and feelings along with the will, heart, and spirit interact for sanctificational growth (see chapter three) as well as true worship.

But authentic worship also includes truth (John 4:24). Truth "is a quality of action, not simply an abstract concept . . . [it is] conformity with the divine reality as revealed in Jesus" which characterizes true worship (Morris, 1995, pp. 261–262), that is, true actions (i.e., actions that match reality) that reflect truth as revealed in Scripture and in Christ. Carson (1991) agrees that the kind of worshiper that the Father seeks, worships him "on the basis of God's incarnate Self–expression, Christ Jesus himself, through whom God's person and will are finally and ultimately disclosed ('in truth')" (p. 225). If the concept of worshipping "in truth" is a reference to the revelation of Jesus Christ who declared himself "the truth" (John 14:6), it seems possible that it could fit the "in-Christ" union motif. This notion may indicate that one essential aspect of true worship is that it is to be conducted from an intimate relationship with Jesus Christ and in "conformity to the divine reality as revealed in Jesus," that is, a life being conformed to the image of Christ (Rom 8:29). True worship helps believers become more like Christ from the foundation of union with Christ. Worship, then, can be considered as the acting out of one's relationship with the Father through Jesus Christ.

Together, "spirit and truth," two characteristics that "form one matrix, indivisible" (Carson, 1991, p. 226) direct worshipers "to the need for complete sincerity and complete reality in [their] approach to God" (Morris, 1995, p. 239) with the whole being. Thus, the believer's whole being— "mind as well as emotions, physique as well as feelings are to combine in God's praise" (Manson, 1988, p. 731). Worship, like sanctification, involves the total human being in all aspects bodily and spiritually, materially and immaterially. Moreland (1997) concurs:

> Jesus taught that we are to worship in spirit and in truth. By this, Jesus meant that *the worship that really counts is not based on external conformance to custom.* Instead, it is to be rooted in the inner being; it should be sincere and earnest; and it out to be in accordance with the true nature of God, His revelation, and His acts. (p. 160)

VIM Related to the Lord's Supper

Perhaps no worship activity fits the theories and models of human participation in this study and provides an excellent example of intentional means as does the eating and drinking that takes place in the Lord's Supper. The significance of participating in the Lord's Supper as presented by Jesus Christ for sanctificational growth can be seen in the following discussion. It seems to be Christ's practical means of keeping the vision of one's life in Christ and of one's relationship with God by regularly and collectively bringing his disciples into the experience of being in his presence and being in union with him.

As Christ ate the Passover meal with his disciples in the upper room (Matt 26:26–29; Mark 14:22–25; Luke 22:14–23), he took bread and later a cup of wine, and distributed them to his followers teaching them the significance of these two elements and his actions. He urged them to "do this in remembrance of me" (Luke 22:19; 1 Cor 11:24) and thus seems to place this "meal" at the heart of one's relationship with him (Smith, 2005, p. 16). From these words, believers are introduced to the relationship of the bodily action of eating and drinking and the spiritual effect of this action.

> This event in the life of the church, the physical act of eating and drinking, was fundamentally a spiritual event. While it was certainly physical eating and drinking that set the stage for the Lord's Supper, it was in the end a symbolic event. Yes, the church did eat and drink, but what was fulfilled were the deepest yearnings of the human soul, that Jesus would enter in and eat with his people. (Smith, p. 16)

But from Christ's words believers are also urged to intentional choice and obedience. The church is to obediently "do this" regularly to remind them of redemption and new life in Christ in the past and for the future. Obedience is a choice. Given free will, making the decision to "commune" with Christ in this way entails the interplay of elements examined in this study such as belief (e.g., meaning of bread and wine) and desire (e.g., acting against or with natural inclinations to "commune" with Christ), personal agency beliefs (e.g., viewing myself in union with Christ) and goals (e.g., Christlikeness), and sanctification (e.g., understanding of spiritual growth) and union with Christ (e.g., death to sin and life in Christ).

As with any spiritual practice, participating in the Lord's Supper is a means to an end. It may be considered not only as a "memorial" to recall Christ's death, burial, and resurrection but also as a means of experiencing his presence. Practical theologian Gordon Smith (2005) writes:

> This holy meal is a memorial of a different kind. It is a recollection and a remembrance that take us into an encounter with the very one whom we remember. . . . [I]n our remembering, we are entering into the most vital and life–giving events of all: the death and resurrection of Christ Jesus. In our remembering, the crucified and risen Christ is in our midst. (p. 39)

Smith seems to be stating that in eating the bread and drinking the cup believers experience the reality of their union with Christ. This experience may be possible due to the metaphorical meaning of the bread and wine that Christ was trying to communicate in his words, "This is my body" and "This is my blood" when referring to the bread and wine. The metaphors of bread and wine are familiar concrete illustrations that sketch a mental image of an abstract idea (i.e.,

Christ's person or being) (see Schreiner and Caneday, 2001, pp. 100–102 for a discussion of biblical metaphors whereby "God conveys heavenly realities by means of earthly analogies").

These two phrases have stimulated much debate throughout church history but it is not my desire to enter that debate here. However, holding to Christ's statements as metaphor seems to limit an interpretation of their meaning. Thus, "this is my body" could be understood as, "the bread means or conveys my body" and "this is my blood" as, "the blood conveys my very life," for in Hebrew thought, the life of a creature resides in its blood (Edwards, 2002, p. 426). It is by accepting the reality of Christ's presence by faith in eating and drinking that the believer experiences fellowship and union with Christ. It seems that here, in the Lord's Supper, was Jesus' appointed means of being present in the hearts and minds of the community of the church.

Not only may the elements convey the presence of Christ, but participation in the meal may picture the believer's union with Christ. It provides an opportunity for believers to be reminded of Christ's death, burial, and resurrection and also to be reminded of their own death, burial, and resurrection in Christ. It is an occasion for believers to "reckon" again their death to sin and life in Christ.

Additionally, as was Paul's concern in 1 Corinthians 11:17–34, it provides an opportunity for the church to demonstrate its unity with Christ and with others in the church. Paul could not commend the Corinthians because the Lord's Supper had become an occasion to demonstrate division (v. 18), humiliation (v. 22), indifference (v. 29), and impatience (v. 33). This contrasts with the oneness of the body (1 Cor 12:12–27) that should be demonstrated.

Thus, the Lord's Supper can be an occasion for the believer's union with Christ to be recognized (i.e., a vision of new life in Christ) for the motivational element towards Christlikeness that it is. Willard's VIM model may be seen as Christ's word regarding the cup ("This cup is the new covenant in my blood") relates to the vision of a new life relationship, i.e., a new covenant, with Christ. His command to obedience and thought ("Do this in remembrance of me") could relate to intention by involving a choice to obey and by engaging the mind to recall Christ's life and redemptive work. His encouragement to do this regularly ("Do this" and "as often as you drink it") may relate to the means of participating in the Lord's Supper itself with the aim of ordering one's heart unto Christlikeness.

Ford's personal agency model may also be seen as believers actually experience their union with Christ and their union with the body of Christ (i.e., the church) and view themselves in both contexts as they eat and drink in Christ's presence together with other members of the body of Christ. When practiced with these models in mind, participation in the Lord's Supper as part of the believer's worship experience seems to be an effective means for sanctificational growth.

VIM, Small Groups, and Sanctificational Growth

As has been acknowledged in this study, progressive sanctification is that ongoing work of God through the Holy Spirit in believers' lives involving their intentional participation. This sanctificational work is carried out not only individually but also in community. The "vision" of life in the community of Christ relates to the relational component of sanctificational growth. Believers are to "love one another" just as Christ has loved them which communicates to all people that these believers are followers of Christ (John 13:34–35). A prominent characteristic of believers is their love for others in the Christian family (1 John 2:9–11). Paul states that entry into the unified relationship with others in Christ is a "calling" that is to be intentionally maintained and developed (Eph 4:1–6). This vision of community and oneness is acknowledged and advocated by Christ (John 17:20–26) and Paul (1 Cor 12:12–31; Eph 2:11–22; Phil 2:1–2; 1 Thess 4:9–12). Sanctificational growth has the opportunity to flourish when a vision of living in the community of Christ. But this vision must be accompanied by means intentionally engaged if growth is to occur.

One expression of community is the small group, which can contribute to the sanctificational growth of those involved if they understand that its goal is spiritual growth and then, with "intention," participate in small-group "means" as an essential member of the community. Whereas participation in corporate worship is primarily service that is directed to God, small group participation emphasizes service to others directed by God. This kind of ministry in community is needed for spiritual growth as examined in the discussion of the believer's union with Christ in the body (pp. 155–158).

Professor and pastor Peter Deison (1994) argues that small groups that are centered on the goal of spiritual formation are crucial for the church.

> If we have made the passionate pursuit of Christ our highest aim, we will see the need of His community with a small group of believers. . . . Spiritual formation grows deeper and stronger through the community of a small group. The healthy environment created in such groups allows lives to change and develop. (p. 278)

The potential for small groups to provide for spiritual growth may be related to the understanding that small groups have their foundation in the Trinity. Professor of practical theology James Davies (2001) states that "God as Being exists in community" and therefore, a small group is a demonstration of God's communal image for humanity (p. 644). One could reason that if Christ lives in community and we are growing to be like him, then we too need to live in community. The theology of the communal relationship among the members of the Trinity may provide one reason for developing small groups in which committed fellowship among the participants is a priority. This understanding of relationships may provide the basis for a small group "vision" which portrays the church in terms of intimacy, relatedness, partnership, or friendship.

Another theological tenet for establishing small groups is suggested by the "in-Christ" concept. Believers in union with Christ enter two types of relationships that small groups have the potential to practically facilitate. These relationships were discussed in chapter five regarding the believer's personal relationship with Christ and the believer's communal relationship with others in the body of Christ. First, an intimate relationship with God through Jesus Christ can be understood and strengthened as the group commits to this goal, brings their concerns and needs in prayer to the Father, studies God's Word with the goal of becoming more like Christ, and ministers as Christ would to those within as well as outside the group. Second, relationships with others in the group as "one with Christ" can be understood and strengthened as group members commit themselves to each other, share their lives with one another, care for one another, and exercise their gifts to build up one another. Small groups are able to picture the interdependence of believers with Christ and with one another so that they are brought to maturity and Christlikeness (Eph 4:11–16). Thus, small groups seem to be an effective environment to facilitate and strengthen the reality of the believer's union with Christ.

The distinctive characteristics of small groups, compared to corporate worship, can be seen practically as a means to encourage sanctificational growth. Professors of practical theology and observers of church life, Glen Martin and Gary McIntosh (1997), claim that there are four distinctives to small groups. First, small groups allow face–to–face direct and personal interaction. Second, small groups are commonly small in number, usually three to twelve members, which benefits face–to–face relationships. Third, small groups meet at a regular time schedule, at least twice a month which encourages commitment and accommodates friendship. Fourth, small groups provide a sense of accountability where concern and responsibility for one another is practiced (p. 37). Small groups that uphold these distinctives have the potential for nurturing spiritual growth. In other words, having these characteristics in place does not automatically result in spiritual growth.

But for a small group to have a strong sense of community which can facilitate sanctificational growth, other elements must be incorporated. Deison (1994) notes these key elements of small group community:

1. Clear purpose (e.g., to grow in Christlikeness)
2. Commitment to each person involved as well as a commitment of each person to the group (e.g., when conflicts in schedule arise, the group takes priority)
3. Strong, loving, serving and accessible leadership, supported with a sense of democratic unity (e.g., modeling Christlikeness by the leadership)
4. Explicitly shared beliefs and values (e.g., agreeing to a "covenant") (p. 273)

With these elements in place, a community can develop which creates an "atmosphere for spiritual formation and is, in fact, a part of it" (p. 277). Deison claims:

> Spiritual formation in small groups is where the whole focus of sanctification can happen. It provides a place where God's truth can be discussed, where the Spirit can speak, and God's people can minister to each other. Jesus

summed it up for us when He said, "Love the Lord your God with all your heart and will all your soul and with all your mind. This is the first and greatest commandment. And the second is like it: love your neighbor as yourself. All the law and the prophets hang on these two commandments" (Matt. 22:37–38). (p. 277)

In other words, this kind of small group has the potential to help believers develop a love for God and others as Christ loved God and others. The desire to be like Christ, an evidence of sanctificational growth, can be manifested in a growing ability to love like he did. Small groups are able to encourage this kind of discipleship when its members are committed to this goal. We can see the relevance of these concepts to Ford's motivational theory. With the goal of sanctificational growth in place, this kind of small group provides a supportive environment where the believer's abilities can be exercised and developed. In the context of a small group where intentional Christlike love and harmony are evident resulting in genuine, caring relationships where members serve one another, spiritual growth is given an opportunity to flourish.

Small groups, therefore, may provide a setting for personal transformation to take place when these components are effectively arranged: 1) Vision – life in the community of Christ; 2) Intention – deciding to participate in a small group and intending to contribute to the spiritual growth of others and one's self by trusting others and being trustworthy; 3) Means – engaging the various practices necessary for small group effectiveness such as listening, studying, caring, submitting, serving, and loving. The small group becomes a "miniature" of the Kingdom or the church.

Not only can the small group itself function within the VIM model, the structure or format of the group and its meetings could be framed by the components of VIM, intention and means. For example, the group may decide to establish a kind of covenant that would deepen the commitment level of the participants. A mutual agreement provides accountability for the members to follow through with their decision to be involved in a growing community of Christ demonstrating life in the kingdom or church. Additionally, certain means could be implemented that would encourage the pursuit of the vision. Such practices as praying together, studying God's Word (e.g., discussion, meditation, memorization), doing acts of service for those in and outside the group, celebrating in worship, and submitting to others in the group would solidify relationships and enhance spiritual growth if the vision of being a kingdom person or living a new life in Christ is kept before the group.

Union with Christ and Practical Implications

In chapter five, I argued that believers are responsible to think of themselves in union with Christ as dead to sin and alive to God thus contributing to their sanctificational growth. It is not only because the "union with Christ" expressions occur so frequently (216 times by Paul, 26 times by John) in Scripture, but also because "union with Christ proves to be a central verity, indeed a touchstone reality of the Christian life and experience" (Demarest, 1997, p. 313), that it is helpful to examine how this concept can be actively experienced in the Christian life.

I have suggested a fit between the union with Christ concept and Ford's personal agency belief concept since both incorporate the evaluation of one's capacities and context. The union with Christ concept also fits Willard's VIM model particularly in the areas of intention and means to live a "new life in Christ." Believers can become competent in living a new life in Christ as they, by the Spirit and God's grace, intend to live this way and develop their inner character towards Christlikeness by implementing means that are effective to this end.

In this section, I will propose some practical ways that the union with Christ concept can be personally and corporately embodied so that it becomes a key element in one's sanctificational growth and personal transformation. As union with Christ moves from concept to reality, the capacity and context for sanctificational growth can be experienced. It will also be understood as an essential component to intentional, Christ-empowered living.

Personal Embodiment

Believers have been brought into union with Christ through the work of the Holy Spirit (1 Cor 12:13). But this union is not only to be a spiritual state or position of the believer but it is also to be the experience of the believer. The doctrine can be put into practice. "Once the new life begins to enter our soul, however, we have the responsibility and opportunity of ever more fully focusing our whole being on it and wholly orienting ourselves toward it" (Willard, 1999, p. 158). This section discusses the practical ways this can be done.

I suggest that the believer's union with Christ can be personally embodied and demonstrated as one engages in spiritual disciplines. When the believer's union with Christ is understood as a supernatural indwelling of the Father and the Son (John 10:30; 14:23) by the Holy Spirit (John 14:16–17; 15:26; 16:7–15), then disciplines for the spiritual life are perceived as activities "undertaken to bring us into more effective cooperation with Christ" and "activities undertaken to make us capable of receiving more of his life and power without harm to ourselves or others" (Willard, 1988, p. 156). Through practices that involve bodily actions such as fasting, solitude, study, or service, the body is being trained to naturally respond and live by the power of the new life in Christ. Willard describes the kind of life that can result from spiritual disciplines.

> When through spiritual disciplines I become able heartily to bless those who curse me, pray without ceasing, to be at peace when not given credit for good deeds I've done, or to master the evil that comes my way, it is because my disciplinary activities have inwardly poised me for more and more interaction with the powers of the living God and his Kingdom. Such is the potential we tap into when we use the disciplines. (p. 157)

Though it is a present reality that the believer is in Christ and Christ is in the believer (John 14:20; 17:21) it is the responsibility of believers, by the

Spirit, to fashion their spirit, soul, and mind to manifest the reality of their identification with Christ. The whole person can be formed by the proper use of spiritual disciplines. Willard (1988) explains:

> What then are the specific roles of the spiritual disciplines? Their role rests upon the nature of the embodied human self – they are to *mold* and *shape* it. And our part in our redemption is, through specific and appropriate activities, to "yield" the plastic substance of which we are made to the ways of that new life which is imparted to us by the "quickening spirit." (p. 92)

What are some specific spiritual practices that will enable the believer to experience the reality of their union with Christ? The believer could begin by meditating on the passages of Scripture that support the union with Christ concept such as John 15:5, 15; Galatians 2:20; Colossians 1:27; 2 Corinthians 5:17 as well as Romans 6:1–14. Professor of New Testament Walt Russell (2000, pp. 88–91) states that meditation involves both thought processes and aspects of speaking. He draws this conclusion from the emphases of two Hebrew words, one meaning "to muse about or consider deeply and at length," and the other meaning to "mutter or speak or read in an undertone." Thus, meditation involves both nonverbal and verbal emphasis wherein believers intentionally allow God's word to abide in them as they "muse and mutter [it] throughout the day."

Willard (1988) recognizes the value of this discipline when he writes, "Here we have an activity of mind and body undertaken with all the strength we have to make our total being cooperate effectively with the divine order" (p. 150). Since God's design for believers includes their relationship with Christ (i.e., union), meditation on this relationship implies a cooperation with God's design. As one who is married meditates on this relationship, so he or she is brought into a greater understanding of its meaning.

Theologian Bruce Demarest (1999) also recognizes the benefits of meditation for spiritual formation (i.e., sanctification). Referring to meditation as "giving *attention* with *intention*," he explains the practice and its results.

> Meditation refocuses us from ourselves and from the world so that we reflect on God's Word, His nature, His abilities, and His works. As we come before the Scriptures, we believe that God has something very personal to say. So we prayerfully ponder, muse, and "chew" the words of Scripture and other Christian writings. . . . The goal is simply to permit the Holy Spirit to activate the life–giving Word of God so that something more of our lives is transformed to bring us, every day, a little closer to the image of Christ. Meditation, when it is effective, engages the whole heart: intellect, intuition, will, affections, and moral sense. (p. 133)

If Demarest's view of meditation is accepted and applied to passages dealing with the believer's union with Christ, then meditation provides the opportunity for the Holy Spirit to "activate the life-giving Word of God" and bring them into closer communion with Christ. It seems necessary, then, for believers to regularly give attention to their intimate, supernatural, and vital union with Christ which results in death to sin and life in Christ.

Could this be an aspect of "reckoning" that Paul expects of believers in Romans 6:11? It seems plausible since "reckon" has been understood to mean to "judge" in a "settled determination to live in the light of Christ's death and in the strength of a power which has already defeated sin's reign in death" (Dunn, 1988a, p. 324). The believer deliberates his or her death to sin and resurrection to life while trusting the Spirit to bring its reality to bear on daily conduct.

If meditation is to have optimal impact on one's heart and daily conduct, it seems best to begin the day in meditation upon a passage from Scripture which can then be recalled throughout the day. What is recalled may be a verse, phrase, thought, or even a word from the passage. It may be helpful to provide "cues" that will act as aids in this recall such as a note on a computer monitor or bathroom mirror. Perhaps a routine daily act such as checking email, opening an office or car door, or prayer before a meal could act as a meditation cue. Some computers and watches can be programmed to produce a sound at regular intervals which could be used as a cue. The biblical thought being meditated upon will assimilate into the believer's character (i.e., set of beliefs and desires) as activities like these are intentionally practiced under the guidance of the Holy Spirit.

Memorization is another effective discipline that enables meditation. By memorizing the above passages the opportunity to meditate on them is enhanced since they can be brought to mind at will. Pastor Donald Whitney (1991) provides a practical discussion of these practices as do Willard (1988), Foster (1998) and Russell (2000).

An in–depth approach to embody union with Christ may come through engaging in the spiritual exercises of Ignatius. Originally written for those who could "retreat" somewhere to follow the Spiritual Exercises of St. Ignatius for three, eight, ten, or thirty days, Andre Ravier (1989) has adapted the exercises for those who have one or two hours a day for a week (or month). The purpose of the exercises is to experience the life of Christ through solitude, confession, prayer, meditation, contemplation, and spiritual direction. Ravier uses the language of Romans 6: 1–14 in describing this "do–it–at–home" spiritual retreat.

> The "retreat" we propose is an "immersion" (*immersion* connotes baptism) into the realities revealed to us by Jesus Christ through his Word, his death, and his Resurrection. In fact, everything comes about between God, who beckons because he is love, and the human heart, which responds favorably to his invitation or rejects it. (p. 18)

One would be wise to enter into this spiritual retreat with a clear understanding of Paul's teaching in Romans 6:1–14 so the exercises can be experienced under the supervision of these truths.

Other disciplines could include an intentional study of the life of Christ with an emphasis on his death and resurrection with application to the believers' own death and resurrection. This would provide a challenge to enter into that death and resurrection. One could also pray the Scriptures such as Paul's prayer in Philippians 3:10–11, "that I may know him and the power of his resurrection, and may share his sufferings, becoming like him in his death, that by any means possible I may attain the resurrection of the dead" (ESV).

Submission is another spiritual discipline that contributes to the believer's sanctificational growth. For example, according to Romans 6:13, believers face a regular choice of either offering themselves and their bodily "members" as "weapons" or "instruments" for unrighteousness or of "presenting" or "yielding" themselves and their bodily members as "weapons" or "instruments" for righteousness. Believers have the responsibility to make a decision. "They can choose to put themselves at God's disposal as those alive from the dead, and their constituent parts as instruments or weapons of righteousness to God" (Dunn, 1988a, p. 350). How can believers offer their bodily members in service?

Willard (1988) regards the following practices as ways of submitting one's body and its members to righteousness.

> I submit my tongue as an instrument of righteousness when I *make* it bless them that curse me and pray for them who persecute me, even though it "automatically" tends to strike and wound those who have wounded me. I submit my legs to God as instruments of righteousness when I engage them in physical labor as service, perhaps carrying a burden the "second mile" for someone whom I would rather let my legs kick. I submit my body to righteousness when I do my good deeds without letting them be known, though my whole frame cries out to strut and crow. (p. 119)

In other words, when faced with a choice of whom to serve, believers have the responsibility to offer their services to the one who now rules them. But this kind of habitual living involves the rigorous training of presenting one's bodily members to God in spiritual disciplines.

Spiritual disciplines can be the means of presenting one's self to God. Willard (1988) states that, "A discipline for the spiritual life is . . . nothing but an activity undertaken to bring us into more effective cooperation with Christ" (p. 156). The disciplines that can help this process are designated as "disciplines of abstinence" (solitude, silence, fasting, frugality, chastity, secrecy, and sacrifice) and "disciplines of engagement" (study, worship, celebration, service, prayer, fellowship, confession, and submission) by Willard (p. 158). Foster (1988) lists 12 disciplines in these categories: 1) Inward disciplines—meditation, prayer, fasting, and study; 2) Outward disciplines—simplicity, solitude, submission, and service; and 3) Corporate disciplines—confession, worship, guidance, and celebration (p. v). The practice of these activities is the practice of putting one's self at God's disposal.

"Presenting our members to God as instruments of righteousness" (Rom 6:13) also includes a submission of our lives to the Holy Spirit. In submitting to God, the believer is also submitting to the Holy Spirit. In union with Christ the believer is in union with the Holy Spirit. As discussed in chapter five, Demarest (1997) states that the apostle Paul equates Christ's indwelling with the Spirit's indwelling.

The apostle comfortably moved between the concept of Christ indwelling the believer (Rom 8:10) and the Spirit indwelling the believer (Rom 8:9, 11[twice]) . . . in the economy of the Godhead the Father and the Son live within us and apply their benefits to us via the Spirit. . . . From a biblical perspective, the Holy Spirit is the Spirit of God . . . and the Spirit of Christ. (p. 331)

The practical benefits of the Holy Spirit's indwelling and the believer's submission to him are varied. However, Issler (2001, p. 160), highlights four significant areas (all of which have a bearing on ministry) for which the Spirit's assistance is needed.

1. The Spirit empowers a deepening relationship with God ("fellowship of the Spirit," Phil 2:1; 2 Cor 13:14). The Spirit makes possible an intimate partnership between believers and Spirit from which the Christian community derives its unity, purpose, affection, and disposition. Only as those involved in ministry deepen in fellowship with God by the Spirit, can they effectively encourage others toward a deepening fellowship.

2. The Spirit empowers Christlike living ("fruit of the Spirit," Gal 5:22). The fruit of the Spirit is Christlikeness. The qualities of love, joy, peace, patience, kindness, goodness, faithfulness, gentleness, and self–control can be modeled and genuinely taught by believers who walk by the Spirit.

3. The Spirit empowers the church to grow together into a healthy and mature Christian community (the "unity of the Spirit," Eph 4:3). The believers' first "calling" is to a conduct marked by humility, gentleness, patience, love, and forbearance in an environment of unity and peace. Ministry "issues" should never destroy the church's oneness.

4. The Spirit empowers the ministry to others ("spiritual gifts," 1 Cor 12:1) and evangelism ("filled with the Holy Spirit and spoke the word of God with boldness," Acts 4:31; see also Acts 1:8). The Spirit gives gifts of ministry to individual believers as he wills for the good of the community (1 Cor 12:7) and for a witness to others through the proclamation of the gospel.

As believers practice the discipline of submission to the Holy Spirit, they are enabled to serve the Lord from a confident dependence on the Spirit and from a maturing relationship with Jesus Christ through the Spirit.

Corporate Embodiment

In the discussion of union with Christ in chapter five, it was noted that there is a corporate aspect of this union brought about by the Holy Spirit. "Christ indwells believers (or the community) by the Holy Spirit," writes Bruce Demarest (1997, p. 330). He continues:

With a collective focus [Paul] wrote to the church at Corinth, "Don't you know that you yourselves are God's temple (*naos*) and that God's Spirit lives in you (*en hymin*)? . . . God's temple (*naos*) is sacred. and you are that temple" (1 Cor 3:16–17). Corporately, the church is the special dwelling–place of God's Spirit (Eph 2:21–22). Again we see that the NT moves comfortably from the idea of the Spirit indwelling individual believers to the Spirit abiding with the church collectively. (p. 331)

By the Spirit, believers are baptized into the "body of Christ" (1 Cor. 12:13), the church. All those in union with Christ are also those indwelt by the Spirit of Christ (Acts 16:7; Phil 1:19; 1 Pet 1:11). Believers are members of the body of Christ and one in Christ by the Spirit. Paul wrote, "For just as the body is one and has many members, and all the members of the body, though many, are one body, so it is with Christ. For in one Spirit we were all baptized into one body—Jews or Greeks, slaves or free—and all were made to drink of one Spirit" (1 Cor 12:12–13) (ESV). Believers are one in Christ spiritually. Paul wrote in Romans 12:4–5, "For as in one body we have many members, and the members do not all have the same function, so we, though many, are one body in Christ, and individually members one of another."

As members of the body of Christ, the church, believers are also united with one another (1 Cor 6:15–17; 12:12–27; Eph 4:4, 15–16; 5:23, 30; Col 1:18). "The essential point is that in spite of their various differences, all true believers are united by the Spirit to Christ and to one another" (Demarest, 1997, p. 342). Thus, we can say that this describes the believers' position or state. However, there must be a practical demonstration of this unity. Some ways this union (i.e., "oneness") can be practiced are now considered.

Richard Foster (1998) delineates four spiritual disciplines as corporate disciplines including confession, worship, guidance, and celebration. These practices help unite the body of Christ and give expression to the church's oneness. Since worship has already been examined, I will briefly focus on the other disciplines.

Confession is both a private ("there is one God and one mediator between God and men, the man Christ Jesus," 1 Tim 2:5) and corporate discipline ("confess your sins to each other and pray for each other," Jas 5:16). Though believers are called "saints" in Scripture, they often do not act like it. Within the community of Christ who is its example of forgiveness, there is the need for both confession and forgiveness.

Paul notes this need in his instructions to the church community at Colossae. In the context of life in Christ (Col 3:1, 3, 11) and having identified these believers as "chosen ones, holy, and beloved" (Col 3:12), he exhorts them to forgive "each other; as the Lord has forgiven you, so you also must forgive" (Col. 3:13) when they have a "complaint against another," that is, "a debt which needs to be remitted" (Rogers & Rogers, 1998, p. 468). Saints still sin, often against other saints, therefore they need to confess their sins that forgiveness might be granted. Foster (1998) expresses the significance of this discipline for the church.

The Discipline of confession brings an end to pretense. God is calling into being a Church that can openly confess its frail humanity and know the forgiving and empowering graces of Christ. Honesty leads to confession, and confession leads to change. May God give grace to the Church once again to recover the Discipline of confession. (p. 157)

Another discipline that expresses the unity of the community of Christ, explained by Foster (1998), is communal guidance. Foster notes that God often led his people through decisions made as a group. God led the children of Israel out of bondage as a people collectively (p. 176). Jesus taught that God would be among the disciples when together and provide discernment of his will (Matt 18:19–20). By the discernment of a community of believers, Paul and Barnabas were set apart to take the gospel to cities in the Roman Empire (Acts 13:13). The first major church issue needing resolution was decided by a gathering of elders and apostles who were given direction by their own experiences and by the Holy Spirit (Acts 15). This was an example of "Spirit–directed unity" (p. 179).

Though not a common practice in many churches, the desire to discern God's will as a whole will lead to the development of methods to accommodate this practice. First, a responsive environment must be in place. Spiritual director Rose Mary Dougherty (1995) states three conditions essential to the life of this kind of group. "Members must agree to commit themselves to 1) an honest relationship with God; 2) wholehearted participation in the group process through prayerful listening and response; and 3) opening their spiritual journeys to the consideration of others" (p. 36).

Though these conditions do not guarantee effective group spiritual direction, they do indicate a willingness of group members to be part of the process.

Spiritual guidance can be more intentional by the formation of a small group for the purpose of group spiritual direction. Spiritual director Jeannette Bakke (2000) suggests that potential members of such a group need to:

1. Agree to participate with each other (3–6 people) for a set length of time at a particular place and at particular intervals
2. Discuss what spiritual direction is and share expectations, intentions, and hopes
3. Agree to protect confidentiality of what is shared in the group
4. Decide on any commitments they wish to make regarding prayer for each other or the practice of Christian disciplines
5. Arrange for leadership responsibility
6. Decide how the group spiritual direction sessions will be organized—structure, environment, time allotments, appropriate feedback guidelines, attentiveness to God and others, other plans (p. 145).

This meeting, at the group's inception, may take the form of a longer meeting (5–6 hours) or even a retreat.

Dougherty (1995, pp. 48–55) outlines a typical meeting pattern. First, the group meets in a larger group (20–30 minutes) for announcements, Scripture reading, prayer (audible and silent), and meditation. This sets the foundation and tone for the entire evening.

Members then move into their small groups in silence. This is followed by a format that is the same for each group.

1. Continued silence (5 minutes) with invitation for someone to share when appropriate
2. Sharing by one person (10–15 minutes)
3. Silence (3–4 minutes) for an awareness of God's presence
4. Response (10 minutes) from group members
5. Silence (5 minutes) to pray for the one who just presented
6. Repeat the process for everyone in the group
7. Prayer for absent member(s) (10 minutes)
8. Reflection on their time together (10 minutes or longer)

Dougherty (1995) understands the relatedness of group spiritual direction and the unity of the Christian community and concludes that:

> spiritual direction is one expression of spiritual community. The dynamism of radical love that animates spiritual community also animates spiritual direction in any form. In spiritual direction two or more people gather in the power of love and for the sake of love. In the arena of love, one is brought face–to–face with the primary discernment of spiritual community: "Do you seek God?" And then, "What does this seeking mean for your life? (p. 14)

Greater detail regarding corporate direction is given by W. Paul Jones (2002, pp. 243–252), a former Wesleyan and present Trappist monk. Along with the spiritual disciplines of prayer, Scripture meditation, sacraments, and fasting, Jones presents Wesley's "Christian conferencing" [*con* = to be able; *confer* = to consult, honor, advise] as "Wesley's way of declaring spiritual direction to be a mandatory means of grace" (p. 85). It was his desire that those receiving spiritual direction would also give it. Jones claims that this is the "heart of direction: *Receiving and giving spiritual direction are intended to form a dynamic whole*" (p. 88). Corporate spiritual direction or guidance can not only express unity, but can also help maintain unity or bring the community of Christ into greater unity.

The early church, as depicted in Acts, demonstrated its "togetherness"—"in one place" (2:1), in prayer (1:14; 4:24), for worship (5:12), for meals and fellowship (2:46), decision–making (15:25), and in glorifying God (Rom 15:6) (Demarest, 1997, p. 343). Through these practices examined here and others that are mentioned, Christian believers can "become outwardly and practically what they are inwardly and spiritually. We need to give loving, tangible expression to the spiritual unity that exists among us in the body of Christ" (Demarest, p. 343).

The last of Foster's (1998) corporate disciplines is the discipline of celebration. The inclusion of this discipline suggests the essential role of emotions in Christian living and sanctificational growth. Foster writes:

> Celebration is at the heart of the way of Christ. He entered the world on a high note of jubilation: "I bring you good news of a great joy," cried the angel, "which shall come to all the people" (Luke 2:10). He left the world bequeathing his joy to the disciples: "These things I have spoken to you that my joy may be in you, and that your joy may be full" (John 15:11). (p. 190)

"Celebration brings joy into life, and joy makes us strong," writes Foster (p. 191). Joy helps sustain all activities including those that involve intense discipline. "Joy is a pervasive sense . . . of well being" that says "all is well" (Willard, 2002, pp. 132–133). Since joy is the end result, "celebration is central to all the Spiritual Disciplines" (p. 191). For believers, the one thing that will produce genuine joy is obedience. Thus,

> joy is the end result of the Spiritual Disciplines functioning in our lives. God brings about the transformation of our lives through the Disciplines, and we will not know genuine joy until there is a transforming work within us. (p. 193)

Foster (pp. 194–195) discusses the nature of joyful celebration and illustrates the interrelatedness of the human capacities connected to Christian living. Paul calls believers to "Rejoice in the Lord always; again I will say, Rejoice" (Phil 4:4). How is this accomplished? Paul continues, "Do not be anxious about anything, but in everything by prayer and supplication with thanksgiving let your requests be known to God." And what results? "And the peace of God, which passes all understanding, will guard your hearts and your minds in Christ Jesus" (Phil 4:6–7). A life of joy and peace begins with a "care–free" approach to living that is free from anxiety as demonstrated by continual prayer and thanksgiving. However, the mind and will are also involved as Paul exhorts believers to intentionally think on things that are true, honorable, just, pure, lovely, commendable, excellent, and worthy of praise (Phil 4:8). Joyful celebration results from an act of the will whereby believers choose to set their minds on what is "good" as described by Paul.

What are some practical ways to express joyful celebration as the people of God? Foster suggests a) singing, dancing, or shouting/making noise; b) laughing; c) enjoying the "creative gifts of fantasy and imagination;" d) making family events into times of celebration and thanksgiving; or e) taking advantage of the festivals of our culture or of our own making (pp. 197–201). Thus, celebration is practiced not only in a church setting, but literally becomes a way of living in Christ.

In confession, worship, guidance, and celebration the body of Christ comes alive, though not "automatically" simply by having these "ministries" in place. These corporate disciplines entail the whole personality of the believer for effective practice. Thus, as the character of individual believers is transformed so is the practice of collective believers transformed. Church ministries must address both levels of transformation for sanctificational growth to result. The tendency of a church might be to focus on the church's programs. However, for the church to truly become the effectively functioning body of Christ God designed, it must address the issues of heart and mind as well as the practical issues. At the very least, the ministries themselves need to be evaluated to determine if they are true to the goal of sanctificational growth.

These disciplines help develop and maintain the corporate aspect of the believer's union with Christ brought about by the Holy Spirit. Corporately, the church is the special dwelling–place of God's Spirit (Eph 2:21–22) enabling the church to worship God and build itself up in love (Eph 4:16). By the Spirit, believers are members of the body of Christ and are one in Christ. As members of the body of Christ, the church, believers are also united with one another (1 Cor 6:15–17; 12:12–27; Eph 4:4, 15–16; 5:23, 30; Col 1:18). This unity can be practically demonstrated as these corporate disciplines are practiced.

Proposals for Further Research

This study has focused on the essentiality of human participation in sanctificational growth. Human participation has been expressed by several facets—intentionality, human capabilities, personal agency beliefs, and character development. However, many other important issues surfaced that could not be addressed.

In relation to Ford's Motivational Systems Theory there are two recommendations for further research. First, this study focused on one component of motivation, personal agency beliefs. However, there are two other components in Ford's motivational theory, goals and emotional arousal, both of which need to be integrated with aspects of sanctification. Related to goals, Professor Steven Porter (2002) addresses the conceptual confusion created by differing terminology used to describe the goal of sanctification such as holiness, Christlikeness, discipleship, righteousness, glorifying God, or godliness. He writes, "Confusion reigns when there is no meta–theory which deals appropriately with divergent theoretical voices" (p. 420). The development of such a theory needs to be researched along with its integration with Ford's understanding of goals or more confusion may result.

The place of emotions as a component of motivation towards and contributor to sanctificational growth needs to be fully addressed as well. As seen in chapter three, Ford claims that emotional arousal is an essential element in motivation and Willard believes that emotions need to be understood and managed that their contribution to spiritual formation can be judged. With a full examination of these components and their corresponding biblical, theological, and philosophical elements, a broader and better understanding of sanctification could result.

Second, brief mention was made of the biblical concept of wisdom in relationship to the skills (i.e., capability) component in Ford's personal agency beliefs. This relationship needs to be researched to examine the strength of the relationship of these two concepts. "Wisdom for living" as skill for effective functioning needs further study.

Related to the doctrine of sanctification, this study focused on sanctificational synergism. Two proposals for further research relate to this concept. First, entailed in sanctificational synergism is a tension between divine and human involvement in sanctification that needs further scrutiny. Further research could lead to the development of a model for synergistic sanctification that more clearly indicates God's involvement and human participation in the sanctificational process. Current models seem inadequate.

Second, in this study, one common element among the views of sanctification was highlighted—synergism. It was demonstrated that all evangelical theories of sanctification supported this concept. However, there may be other common elements among these theories. By extracting, examining, and comparing these common elements perhaps scholarship can develop a "macro-theory" for sanctification or at least a consensus among the views. Efforts have been made to distinguish theories of sanctification (Gundry, 1987; Alexander, 1988). Perhaps, similar efforts could be made to demonstrate their unity.

Finally, I have touched upon some aspects of free will in relationship to sanctificational growth. One issue that was raised in this discussion was the notion of the renewal of the will after conversion. Lewis and Demarest (1996) postulate the idea that different states of human nature affect the power of self-determination: (1) prior to the Fall—human power of contrary choice, God knows all things, (2) after the Fall—God foreknows that people with depraved natures use their power of self–determination only sinfully so He chose the elect to repentance and granted them a new heart, (3) after regeneration—believers have the power of contrary choice again, and (4) after glorification—believers will no longer be able to sin (p. 357, Vol. 1). Whether this explanation is acceptable or not can be debated. But it may indicate that one's view of the power of the will at these stages contributes to one's view of sanctification. The relationship of the pre–regenerated and post–regenerated will needs further research as it relates to human participation in sanctificational growth. Perhaps a study of the relationship of the will and progressive sanctification would be beneficial.

Conclusion

Presently, as Christian education establishes itself as an academic discipline, there is debate and concern over the changing role of the Bible and theology related to the influence of the social sciences on the field. I hope that the commitment of this book to sound theological and biblical understanding informed by relevant philosophical and psychological concepts related to spiritual growth provides not only a valuable contribution to the field but also provides an example of the primacy of God's Word in these matters related to Christian education.

Additionally, I hope this study illustrates the feasibility of maintaining the connection of academic efforts to the life of the church. My life has been personally enriched by this study and this has enriched the life the church I pastor. As I have sought new evidence, questioned beliefs, and persevered in research and writing, I have been compelled to practice what I have written which has been an example to those under my care. The deepening of my own understanding of sanctificational growth has had a positive affect on others.

According to Christian educator James Wilhoit (2005), a transition is taking place in the field of Christian education from its current conceptual understanding towards a spiritual formation paradigm. But he expresses concern.

> One cannot deny that there has been a growing shift in language from Christian education to spiritual formation. However, it is not clear that there has really been a commensurate conceptual shift.

> At the moment spiritual formation remains far more of a connotative slo-
> gan than a precise descriptor. It speaks of a desire to favor nurture over sociali-
> zation, to set grace at the center of spiritual growth, to accentuate the need for
> community, and to place emphasis on head and heart. All these are worthy as-
> pirations, but lacking a good theory, this may remain as little more than an
> enlightened slogan. Simply adopting the language of spiritual formation will
> not automatically give the academic field of CE the foundations and direction it
> needs for this time of transition. (p. 403)

My desire is that this study will contribute some "good theory" to the field
so that at least a slight conceptual shift can accompany the language of spiritual
formation. If Christian education is in transition towards adopting concepts from
spiritual formation, I would like to enter the conversation through this study,
continue to learn from others, and help facilitate the process.

Perhaps the failure of Christian educators to encourage the sanctificational
growth of members of the body of Christ indicates a loss or confusion of purpose. I fear this confusion of vision has occurred in many pastoral-educational
settings. A commitment to sanctificational growth personally and in ministry by
those in the classroom or in the church would contribute to the strengthening of
the academy as well as the church.

Do believers have reason to believe they can progress in sanctificational
growth? The following are principles from this study that support the idea that
believers can grow spiritually.

1. God has provided the essential resources. Sanctification is a work of
   God in which he has provided by the Word and Spirit and in the
   church corporately and individually (e.g., leadership, teaching,
   preaching) the resources necessary for spiritual growth.
2. Believers participate in their spiritual growth. Sanctification takes
   place as believers accept the responsibility to cooperate with God in
   the synergistic process of sanctificational growth.
3. Believers possess the God–given ability to intentionally engage in
   their spiritual growth. They are endowed with the ability to make free
   choices, within a transformed character under the direction of the
   Holy Spirit, that nurture sanctificational growth.
4. Believers are able to develop motivation. Motivation for sanctificational growth comes from establishing the goal of spiritual growth,
   giving emotions a place of regulating and energizing spiritual
   growth, and primarily (for this study) determining that in the believer's union with Christ is provided the capability and context for
   spiritual growth.
5. Believers are able to appropriate resources. Believers are able to deliberately choose for themselves from the spiritual resources and
   practical means that union with Jesus Christ (and thus in the Spirit)
   provides, so that they will live as dead to sin and alive to God in the
   realm of new life.
6. Believers corporately (i.e., the church) are an agency for sanctificational growth as they envision their "new life in Christ," develop

strategies and ministries with the intention to facilitate Christlike-ness, and implement effective means for sanctificational growth.

This study has suggested that human participation is essential to sanctifica-tion. I addressed the nature of sanctificational growth by proposing an essential synergistic component (i.e., both God and believers participate) that dynamically operates within the believer. We saw that human participation involves the be-liever's responsibility to believe they have the ability, drawing upon God's re-sources, for sanctificational growth. The effectiveness of spiritual growth de-pends at some level on understanding intention (i.e., the power to decide) and its part in the Christian's belief structure. An element of the Christians' belief struc-ture is their view of themselves as capable of and supported in (i.e., personal agency beliefs) their quest of sanctificational growth. Additionally, this study suggested a "loose" fit of these personal agency beliefs with the Pauline motif of union with Christ. I also suggested a fit between Willard's VIM model empha-sizing intentionality with Romans 6:1–14. These exercises suggest, and act as examples of, the integrative coherency of these concepts.

BIBLIOGRAPHY

Alexander, D. L. (Ed.). (1988). *Christian spirituality: Five views of sanctification.* Downers Grove, IL: InterVarsity.

Anthony, M. J. (2001). Worship. In M. J. Anthony (Ed.), Evangelical dictionary of Christian education (pp. 730–731). Grand Rapids, MI: Baker.

Arndt, W. F. & Gingrich, F. W. (1979). A Greek-English lexicon of the new testament and other early Christian literature. Chicago: University of Chicago.

Bakke, J. A. (2000). Holy invitations: Exploring spiritual direction. Grand Rapids, MI: Baker.

Bandura, A. (1977a). Social learning theory. Englewood Cliffs, NJ: Prentice Hall.

Bandura, A. (1977b). Self-efficacy: Toward a unifying theory of behavior change. Psychological Review, 84, 191–215.

Bandura, A. (1982). Self-efficacy mechanism in human agency. American Psychologist, 37, 122–147.

Bandura, A. (1989). Self-regulation of motivation and action through internal standards and goal systems. In L A. Pervin (Ed.), Goal concepts in personality and social psychology (pp. 19–85). Hillsdale, NJ: Lawrence Erlbaum.

Bandura, A. & Schunk, D. H. (1981). Cultivating competence, self-efficacy, and intrinsic interest through proximal self-motivation. Journal of Personality and SocialPsychology, 46, 610–620.

Barrett, C. K. (1968). The first epistle to the Corinthians. Peabody, MA: Hendrickson.

Bartsch, H. W. (1991). λογίζομαι. In H. Balz & G. Schneider (Eds.), Exegetical dictionary of the new testament, vol. 2 (pp. 354–355). Grand Rapids, MI: Eerdmans.

Beasley-Murray, G. R. (1993). Dying and rising with Christ. In G. F. Haw-thorne, R. P. Martin, & D. G. Reid (Eds.), Dictionary of Paul and his letters (pp. 218–222). Downers Grove, IL: InterVarsity.

Belleville, L. (1996). 2 Corinthians. Downers Grove, IL: InterVarsity.

Berkhof, L. (1933). Manual of reformed doctrine. Grand Rapids, MI: Eerdmans.

Best, E. (1972). The first and second epistles to the Thessalonians. Peabody, MA: Hendrickson.

Beyreuther, E. (1976). Joy, Rejoice. In C. Brown (Ed.), The new international dictionary of new testament theology, vol. 2. (pp. 352–361). Grand Rapids, MI: Zondervan.

Boa, K. (2001). Conformed to his image: Biblical and practical approaches to spiritual lformation. Grand Rapids, MI: Zondervan.

Brower, K. E. (1996). Sanctification, Sanctify. In I. H. Marshall, A. R. Millard, J. I. Packer, & D. J. Wiseman (Eds.), New bible dictionary (3rd ed.) (pp. 1057–1059). Downers Grove, IL: InterVarsity.

Bruce, F. F. (1982). The epistle to the Galatians. Grand Rapids, MI: Eerdmans.

Carter, C. W. (1983). A contemporary Wesleyan theology: Biblical, systematic, and practical, vol. 1. Grand Rapids, MI: Francis Asbury Press.

Carson, D. A. (1991). The gospel according to John. Grand Rapids, MI: Eerd-mans.

Chafer, L. S. (1948). Systematic theology. Dallas: Dallas Seminary Press.

Chan, S. (1998). Spiritual theology: A systematic study of the Christian life. Downers Grove, IL: InterVarsity.

Ciocchi, D. M. (1993). Human freedom. In J. P. Moreland & D. M. Ciocchi (Eds.), Christian perspectives on being human: A multidisciplinary ap-proach to integration. Grand Rapids, MI: Baker.

Clement, D. E. (2001). Integration of faith and science. In M. J. Anthony (Ed.), Evangelical dictionary of Christian education (pp. 365–366). Grand Rapids, MI: Baker.

Danker, F. W. (Ed.). (2000). A Greek-English lexicon of the New Testament and other early Christian literature (3rd ed.). Chicago: The University of Chicago Press.

Davids, P. H. (1990). The first epistle of Peter. Grand Rapids, MI: Eerdmans.

Davies, J. A. (2001). Small groups. In M. J. Anthony (Ed.), Evangelical dictionary of Christian education (pp. 644–645). Grand Rapids, MI: Baker.

Deasley, A. R. G. (1996). Legalism. In W. A. Elwell (Ed.), Evangelical dictionary of biblical theology (pp. 478–479). Grand Rapids, MI: Baker.

Deison, P. V. (1994). Spiritual formation through small groups. In K. O. Gangel and J. C. Wilhoit (Eds.), The Christian educator's handbook on spiritual formation (pp. 269– 279). Grand Rapids, MI: Baker.

Demarest, B. (1997). The cross and salvation: The doctrine of salvation. Wheaton, IL: Crossway.

Demarest, B. (1999). Satisfy your soul: Restoring the heart of Christian spirituality. Colorado Springs, CO: NavPress.

Dougherty, R. M. (1995). Group spiritual direction: Community for discernment. Mahwah, NJ: Paulist.

Dunn, J. D. G. (1988a). Word biblical commentary: Romans 1–8. Dallas, TX: Word.

Dunn, J. D. G. (1988b) Word biblical commentary: Romans 9–16. Dallas, TX: Word.

Dunn, J. D. G. (1996). The epistles to the Colossians and to Philemon. Grand Rapids, MI: Eerdmans.

Edwards, J. R. (2002). The gospel according to Mark. Grand Rapids, MI: Eerdmans.

Erickson, M. J. (1985). Christian theology. Grand Rapids, MI: Baker.

Fee, G. D. (1987). The first epistle to the Corinthians. Grand Rapids, MI: Eerdmans.

Fee, G. D. (1994). God's empowering presence: The Holy Spirit in the letters of Paul. Peabody, MA: Hendrickson.

Fee, G. D. (1995). Paul's letter to the Philippians. Grand Rapids, MI: Eerdmans.

Ferguson, S. B. (1988). The reformed view. In D. L. Alexander (Ed.), Christian spirituality: Five views of sanctification (pp. 47–76). Downers Grove, IL: InterVarsity.

Fetters, L. S. (1992). The Holy Spirit in sanctification. In Fetters, P.R. (Ed.), Theological perspectives: Arminian-Wesleyan reflections on theology. The Church of the United Brethren in Christ.

Fitzmyer, J. A. (1967). Pauline theology: A brief sketch. Englewood Cliffs, NJ: Prentice Hall.

Ford, M. E. (1992). Motivating humans: Goals, emotions, and personal agency beliefs. Newbury Park, CA: Sage.

Forde, G. O. (1988). The Lutheran view. In Alexander, D. L. (Ed.), Christian spirituality: Five views of sanctification (pp. 13–32). Downers Grove, IL: InterVarsity.

Foster, R. (1998) Celebration of discipline: The path to spiritual growth (3rd ed.). San Francisco: HarperSanFrancisco.

Frame, J. M. (2002). The doctrine of God. Phillipsburg, NJ: P & R Publishing.

Friesen, G. (1980). Decision making and the will of God. Portland, OR: Multnomah.

Gaffin, R. B. (1988). New creation, new creature. In W. A. Elwell (Ed.), Encyclopedia of the Bible, vol. 3. Grand Rapids, MI: Baker.

Gangel, K. (2001). Integration of theology and educational philosophy. In M. J. Anthony (Ed.), Evangelical dictionary of Christian education (pp. 366–368). Grand Rapids, MI: Baker.

Garrett, J. L., Jr. (1995). Systematic theology: Biblical, historical, and evangelical, vol. 2. Grand Rapids, MI: Eerdmans.

Geen, R. G. (1995). Human motivation: A social psychological approach. Belmont, CA: Brooks/Cole.

Gingrich, F. W. (1983). Shorter lexicon of the Greek new testament (2nd ed.) (Rev. ed.). Chicago: University of Chicago Press.

Goetzmann, J. (1978). Wisdom, folly, philosophy. In C. Brown (Ed.), The new international dictionary of new testament, vol. 3 (pp. 1023–1033). Grand Rapids, MI: Zondervan.

Goldberg, L. (1980). חכם (hakam) be wise, act wise(ly). In R. L. Harris, G. L. Archer, & B. K. Waltke (Eds.), Theological wordbook of the old testament (pp. 282–284). Chicago: Moody.

Gorman, M. J. (2001). Cruciformity: Paul's narrative spirituality of the cross. Grand Rapids, MI: Eerdmans.

Green, G. L. (2002). The letters to the Thessalonians. Grand Rapids, MI: Eerdmans.

Grudem, W. (1994). Systematic theology: An introduction to biblical doctrine. Grand Rapids, MI: Zondervan.

Gundry, S. N. (Ed.). (1987). Five views on sanctification. Grand Rapids, MI: Zondervan.

Guthrie, D. (1981). New testament theology. Downers Grove, IL: InterVarsity.

Harner, N. C. (1939). The educational work of the church. New York: Abingdon-Cokesbury.

Hawthorne, G. F. (1983). Philippians. Waco, TX: Word.

Heppe, H. (1978). Reformed dogmatics (Rev. ed.) (G. T. Thomson, Trans.). Grand Rapids, MI: Baker.

Hodge, C. (1946). Systematic theology, vol. 3. Grand Rapids, MI: Eerdmans.

Hoehner, H. W. (2002). Ephesians: An exegetical commentary. Grand Rapids, MI: Baker.

Hoekema, A. A. (1987).The reformed perspective. In S. N. Gundry (Ed.), Five views on sanctification (pp. 61–90). Grand Rapids, MI: Zondervan.

Holy Bible: English standard version. (2001). Wheaton, IL: Crossway Bibles.

Hubbard, M. V. (2002). New creation in Paul's letters and thought. Cambridge: Cambridge University Press.

Issler, K. (2000). A model of character reformation. Unpublished paper.

Issler, K. (2001). Wasting time with God: A Christian spirituality of friendship with God. Downers Grove, IL: InterVarsity.

Issler, K., & Habermas, R. (1994). How we learn: A Christian teacher's guide to educational psychology. Grand Rapids, MI: Baker.

Jones, W. P. (2002). The art of spiritual direction: Giving and receiving spiritual guidance. Nashville, TN: Upper Room.

Kelly, J. N. D. (1969). The epistles of Peter and of Jude. Peabody, MS: Hendrickson.

Knight, G. W. (1992). The pastoral epistles. Grand Rapids, MI: Eerdmans.

Kraft, C. H. (1979). Christianity in culture: A study in dynamic biblical theologizing in cross-cultural perspective. Mary Knoll, NY: Orbis.

Kraft, C. H. (1989). Christianity with power: Your worldview and your experience of the supernatural. Ann Arbor, MI: Vine Books.

Kraft, C. H. (2001). Culture, communication and Christianity. Pasadena, CA: William Cary Library.

Kruse, C. G. (2000). The letters of John. Grand Rapids, MI: Eerdmans.

Kuyper, A. (1900). The work of the Holy Spirit (H. De Vries, Trans.). Grand Rapids, MI: Eerdmans.

Levison, J. R. (1993). Creation and New Creation. In G. F. Hawthorne & R. P. Martin (Eds.), Dictionary of Paul and his letters. Downers Grove, IL: InterVarsity.

Lewis, G. R. & Demarest, B. A. (1996). Integrative theology. Grand Rapids, MI:Zondervan.

Longenecker, R. N. (1990). Galatians. Dallas: Word.

Manson, P. D. (1988). Worship. In S. B. Ferguson & D. F. Wright (Eds.), New dictionary of theology (pp. 730–732). Downers Grove, IL: InterVarsity.

Marshall, I. H. (1978). The epistles of John. Grand Rapids, MI: Zondervan.

Marshall, I. H. (1996a). Salvation. In S. B. Ferguson, D. F. Wright, & J. I. Packer (Eds), New dictionary of theology (pp. 610–611). Downers Grove, IL: InterVarsity.

Marshall, I. H. (1996b). Worship. In I. H. Marshall, A. R. Millard, J. I. Packer, & D. J. Wiseman (Eds.), New bible dictionary (3rd ed.) (p. 1250). Downers Grove, IL: InterVarsity.

Martin, R. P. (1986). 2 Corinthians. Waco, TX: Word.

Martin, G., & McIntosh, G. (1997). Creating community: Deeper fellowship through small group ministry. Nashville, TN: Broadman & Holman.

McGrath, A. E. (1999). Christian spirituality. Oxford: Blackwell.

McQuilkin, J. R. (1987). The Keswick perspective. In Gundry, S. N. (Ed.), Five views on sanctification (pp. 149–183). Grand Rapids, MI: Zondervan.

Mellick, R. R., Jr. (1991). Philippians, Colossians, Philemon. Nashville, TN: Broadman.

Moo, D. (1996). The epistle to the Romans. Grand Rapids, MI: Eerdmans.

Moo, D. J. (2000). The letter of James. Grand Rapids, MI: Eerdmans.

Moreland, J. P. (1997). Love your God with all your mind: The role of reason in the life of the soul. Colorado Springs, CO: NavPress.

Moreland, J. P. & Craig, W. L. (2003). Philosophical foundations for a Christian worldview. Downers Grove, IL: InterVarsity.

Moreland, J. P., & Rae, S. B. (2000). Body & soul: Human nature & the crisis in ethics. Downers Grove, IL: InterVarsity Press.

Morris, L. (1988). The epistle to the Romans. Grand Rapids, MI: Eerdmans.

Morris, L. (1991). The first and second epistles to the Thessalonians. Grand Rapids, MI: Eerdmans.

Morris, L. (1995). The gospel according to John (Rev. ed.). Grand Rapids, MI: Eerdmans.

Mounce, W. D. (1993). The analytical lexicon to the Greek new testament. Grand Rapids, MI: Zondervan.

Murray, J. (1962). Sanctification (the law). In Henry, C. F. H. (Ed.), Basic Christian doctrines. Grand Rapids, MI: Baker.

Mulholland, M. R. (1993). Invitation to a journey. Downers Grove, IL: InterVarsity.

Naugle, D. K. (2002). Worldview: The history of a concept. Grand Rapids, MI: Eerdmans.

O'Brien, P. T. (1991). The epistle to the Philippians. Grand Rapids, MI: Eerdmans.

Oden, T. O. (1994). Life in the Spirit: Systematic theology: Volume Three. New York: HarperSanFrancisco.

Packer, J. I. (1994). Growing in Christ. Wheaton, IL: Crossway.

Palmer, M. D. (1998). Elements of a Christian worldview. In M. D. Palmer (Ed.), Elements of a Christian worldview. Springfield, MO: Logion Press.

Pazmiño, R. W. (1997). Foundational issues in Christian education: An introduction in evangelical perspective (2nd ed.). Grand Rapids, MI: Baker.

Peterson, D. (1995). Possessed by God: A new testament theology of sanctification and holiness. Downers Grove, IL: InterVarsity.

Pieper, F. (1953). Christian dogmatics, vol. 3. St. Louis, MO: Concordia.

Pink, T. (1998). The Will. In E. Craig (Ed.), Routledge encyclopedia of philosophy (vol. 9). (pp. 720–725). New York: Routledge.

Pojman, L. P. (1986). Religious belief and the will. New York: Routledge & Kegan Paul.

Pojman, L. P. (Ed.). (1991). Introduction to philosophy: Classical and contemporary readings. Belmont, CA: Wadsworth.

Porter, S. E. (1993). Holiness, sanctification. In G. F. Hawthorne, R. P. Martin, & D. G. Reid (Eds.), Dictionary of Paul and his letters (pp. 397–402). Downers Grove, IL: InterVarsity.

Porter, S. L. (2002). On the renewal of interest in the doctrine of sanctification: a methodological reminder. Journal of Evangelical Theological Society, 45, 415–426.

Ravier, A. (1989). A do-it-at-home retreat: The spiritual exercises of St. Ignatius of Loyola. San Francisco: Ignatius.

Rightmore, R. D. (1996). Union with Christ. In W. A. Elwell (Ed.), Evangelical dictionary of biblical theology (pp. 789–792). Grand Rapids, MI: Baker.

Rogers, C. L., Jr., & Rogers, C. L., III (1998). The new linguistic and exegetical key to the Greek New Testament. Grand Rapids, MI: Zondervan.

Russel, W. (2000). Playing with fire: How the Bible ignites change in your soul. Colorado Springs, CO: Navpress.

Ryrie, C. C. (1982). Contrasting views on sanctification. In D. K. Campbell (Ed.), Walvoord: A tribute. Chicago: Moody.

Sanders, E. P. (1977). Paul and Palestinian Judaism. Philadelphia: Fortress.

Schmitz, E. D. (1976). γινώσκω. In C. Brown, The new international dictionary of new testament theology, vol. 2 (pp. 392–406). Grand Rapids, MI: Zondervan.

Schneider, J. (1978). σώζω. In C. Brown, The new international dictionary of new testament theology, vol. 3 (pp. 205–216). Grand Rapids, MI: Zondervan.

Schreiner, T. R. (1998). Romans. Grand Rapids, MI: Baker.

Schreiner, T. R., & A. B. Caneday (2001). The race set before us: A biblical theology of perseverance & assurance. Downers Grove, IL: InterVarsity.

Schweitzer, A. (1931). The mysticism of the Apostle Paul. London: Black.

Seebass, H. (1976). Holy, Consecrate, Sanctify, Saints, Devote. In C. Brown (Ed.), Dictionary of new testament theology, vol. 2 (pp. 223–229). Grand Rapids, MI: Zondervan.

Shedd, W. G. T. (1888). Dogmatic theology, vol 2. Grand Rapids, MI: Zondervan.

Shedd, W. G. T. (2003). Dogmatic theology (3rd ed.). A. Gomes (Ed.). Phillipsburg, NJ: Presbyterian and Reformed Publishing.

Silva, M. (1988). Sanctification. In W. A. Elwell (Ed.), Baker encyclopedia of the bible, vol. 4, (pp. 1898–1902). Grand Rapids, MI: Baker.

Sire, J. W. (1997). The universe next door: A basic worldview catalog (3rd ed.). Downers Grove, IL: InterVarsity.

Sire, J. W. (2004). Naming the elephant. Downers Grove, IL: InterVarsity.

Smith, G. T. (2005). A holy meal: The Lord's supper in the life of the church. Grand Rapids, MI: Baker.

Spittler, R. P. (1988). The Pentecostal view. In Alexander, D. L., Christian spirituality: Five views of sanctification, (pp. 133–154). Downers Grove, IL: InterVarsity.

Strong, A. A. (1907). Systematic theology. Old Tappan, NJ: Fleming H. Revell.

Strawson, G. (1998). Free Will. In E. Craig (Ed.), Routledge encyclopedia of philosophy, vol. 3. New York: Routledge.

Swinburne, R. (1997). The evolution of the soul (Rev. ed.). New York: Oxford.

Swinburne, R. (1998). Providence and the problem of evil. Oxford: Clarendon.

Swinburne, R. (2001). Epistemic justification. Oxford: Clarendon.

Thomas, G. (2000). Sacred pathways. Grand Rapids, MI: Zondervan.

Thomas, W. H. G. (1930). The principles of theology: An introduction to the thirty–nine articles. New York: Longman's, Green and Co.

Ury, M. W. (1996). Will. In W. A. Elwell (Ed.), Evangelical dictionary of biblical theology. Grand Rapids, MI: Baker.

van Inwagen, P. (1993). An essay on free will. Oxford: Clarendon.

Vincent, M. R. (1897). A critical and exegetical commentary on the epistles to the Philippians and to Philemon. Edinburgh: T & T Clark.

Walters, G, & Milne, B. A. (1996). Salvation. In I. H. Marshall, A. R. Millard, J. I. Packer, & D. J. Wiseman (Eds.), New bible dictionary (3rd ed.) (pp. 1046–1050). Downers Grove, IL: InterVarsity.

Walvoord, J. F. (1987). The Augustinian–dispensational perspective. In S. N. Gundry (Ed.), Five views on sanctification (pp. 199–226). Grand Rapids, MI: Zondervan.

Wanamaker, C. A. (1990). The epistles to the Thessalonians: A commentary on the Greek text. Grand Rapids, MI: Eerdmans.

Whitney, D. S. (1991). Spiritual disciplines for the Christian life. Colorado Springs: CO: Navpress.

Wilhoit, J. C. (2005). Nothing less than a sea change. Christian Education Journal, 2, 400–404.

Willard, D. (1988). The spirit of the disciplines: Understanding how God changes lives. New York: HarperSanFrancisco.

Willard, D. (1998). Divine conspiracy: Rediscovering our hidden life in God. New York: HarperSanFrancisco.

Willard, D. (1999). Hearing God: Developing a conversational relationship with God. Downers Grove, IL: InterVarsity.

Willard, D. (2002). Renovation of the heart: Putting on the character of Christ. Colorado Springs, CO: NavPress.

Williams, D. E. (2001). Christian education. In M. J. Anthony (Ed.), Evangelical dictionary of Christian education (pp. 132–134). Grand Rapids, MI: Baker.

Williams, J. R. (1990). Renewal theology: Salvation, the Holy Spirit, and Christian living. Grand Rapids, MI: Zondervan.

Wood, L. W. (1988). The Wesleyan view. In Alexander, D. L. (Ed.), Christian spirituality: Five views of sanctification (pp. 95–118). Downers Grove, IL: InterVarsity.

Zuck, R. B. (1998). Spirit–filled teaching: The power of the Holy Spirit in your ministry. Nashville, TN: Word.

INDEX

SCRIPTURE INDEX

ABOUT THE AUTHOR

Keith Kettenring earned his Ph. D. from Biola University/Talbot School of Theology in the field of Christian Education with an emphasis on Christian spirituality. His interest in sanctification and spiritual formation has characterized his pastoral ministry of 25 years. His is committed to teaching and writing about issues entailed in spiritual growth in order to build up the body of Christ and in order to stimulate the believer's understanding of (and engagement in) the process.

He was born into a dedicated Christian family and committed his life to Christ by faith as a young boy. His family served the Lord in Bible colleges, local church ministries, and mission endeavors both in the United States and Jamaica. This background allowed him the opportunity to develop his interests in music, sports, Bible study, theology, and church ministry which were expanded in college (Tennessee Temple University) and seminary (Temple Theological Seminary). He has sought to stay grounded in church ministry while pursuing his educational goals. The loss of his library, notes, and significant materials in a church fire helped direct his life to serious consideration of spiritual formation personally and for the church. He has served Calvary Baptist Church in Anaheim, CA for over 20 years as pastor, worship leader, teacher/educator, and small group leader. Ministry has included frequent trips to Russia to teach in Bible institutes across that country.

He enjoys his marriage to Rhonda (29 years), his two children, Nate and Jenna, and the family dogs, Savanna and Simba. He likes good music, stimulating books, beautiful scenery, a skilled soccer match, a neat house, and quite times.